C.O.P.S.

Crazy Unofficial Police Stories

Charles Lee Brace

Dedication

FOR MY FAMILY AND loving wife, who has been my strength and guide throughout this journey. A special thanks to Massachusetts, Worcester Police Sgt. Andrew (PO-PO) Harris and Sgt. Spencer Tatum whose strength and perseverance stand head and shoulders above the rest of us.

Thanks to Sgt. Angelo Naples (you were right about so many things), Sgt. Paul Wright, Captain James Nissan, Lt. Paul Lukes, Lt. Timothy O'Connor, Detective Samuel Bracey, Detective Daniel Rosario, Officer John Grady, Officer Karen Shea, Detective David Logan, Officer William Lamothe, and Officer Donald Carlson whose examples, mentoring, and training affected me in ways too numerous to mention. A special thanks to Officer John Vassar (my trusted friend who always helped me find my way back)…

For all the rest, my extended police family both past and present, "I will miss you clowns, but NOT the circus. Always remember rank is not a whip, it's a responsibility to those under your command. The officers you command are a reflection of you. Respect them and treat them fairly without bias. They can do remarkable things when you do."

About the Author

C harles Brace, a native of Worcester, Massachusetts, has come a long way from being born in the city elevator. It's this same can't-wait-to-get-here attitude that drove him to write this book.

Charles spent twenty-eight years as a Police Officer, Training Officer, Self-Defense Instructor, Motivational Speaker, Singer, Youth Counselor, and Community Activist. During his life, these are some of the many hats he's worn over the years. But why become a cop? Because people need help, and in most cases, you have to have a big heart and be as nutty as a snickers bar to get them that help.

Charles has a Bachelor's degree in Criminal Justice from Curry College and graduated magna cum laude. Weird, funny, and out of control are the hallmarks of his life as you will see when you read these pages. So, take a moment to grab a coffee, put up your feet, and enjoy glimpses of what it means to be a cop.

Author's Note:

The stories in this book focus on the bizarre and weird side of life and the job of a police officer. They are meant to entertain while giving the reader a view of how strange the human condition can be. Except for one story – which delves into the darker side of policing, they are lighthearted, full of action, and humor when looked at with the right lens.

Chapter One

What It's Like Being a Police Officer

L ife is a series of unexpected events that shock and surprise you — it's the allure of the unexpected adding to its spiciness. Being a Police Officer is like skydiving. Each time, it's new and different, you never know what to expect when you jump. You try not to think about it, you just jump — or more often than not, you are pushed out.

Imagine if you will, you're in an airplane some 45,000 feet above the earth and preparing for your first high altitude skydive. You have your parachute on and the door opens. Suddenly, you launch yourself from the plane and feel the rush of air as you free fall. There is a sense of exhilaration as the flow of air ignites your every sense.

40,000 feet.

35,000 feet.

Finally, you pull the rip cord and all hell breaks loose. The chute doesn't open. You're tumbling, spinning, somersaulting wildly, and your heart pounds in your chest like an invisible hammer. There is a lump in your throat as you vainly struggle to comprehend what is happening.

"Oh… my God! Oh God!" streams from your lips like a wild river as the ground rushes toward you. Your muscles tighten into knots as you strain to pull the chute release. Clutching at the cord, you pull with all your strength but the chute won't release. "Jesus!"

Franticly, you thrust your hand into a multi-pocketed vest seeking salvation by way of a Swiss army knife you've always carried for good luck. It's hard to focus, to control that heavy blanket of smothering fear crushing your fractured mind. Then, in a split moment of fate, your trembling hand grasps a rather small piece of steel. You pull it out and flip open the blade. The task of cutting the tangled rigging and releasing the chute is possible, if only you can get to it in time. "Two straps, just two," echoes in your mind as you hack and saw at the first strap.

30,000 feet.

25,000 feet.

The many cords of the chute swim around your face lashing you like a braided whip. The chute has become a living thing with its many tentacles clutching, clawing, dragging you downward to embrace the cold hard earth below.

20,000 feet.

The desert floor comes into focus like a mirage through watery eyes, its finality stalking you. The moment that we each must embrace at the end is approaching you with the certainty of nightfall, arms outstretched, beckoning you to a cold and painful oblivion. Then — Success! The last of the two straps yield to your Swiss army knife and flutter free from your harness.

15,000 feet.

13,000 feet.

Somewhere within the tumbling madness your tongue detects a salty taste in your mouth, and you feel something wet running out of your nose and across the side of your face. Vertigo begins to cloud your senses as you drift in and out of consciousness. You struggle against the involuntary sleep which closes in on your mind. To sleep is to die! So you fight, willing yourself to remain alert although everything in your waking mind wants to shut down, to embrace the quiet sleep before the end.

Suddenly, there is a sharp pain in your ears and then silence as darkness engulfs you in a lazy mist. In a last effort to preserve your life, a hand drunkenly swipes at a dangling D-ring. Nothing! Then as if in a dream, you manage to pull the emergency chute.

A red and blue plume streams skyward scooping air, slowing your rocketing decent. Wiping the wetness from your nose and mouth you notice the crimson fluid dripping from your fingertips. A sigh of relief escapes your quivering lips.

"Oh, sweet Jesus! Oh God!" you blurt out.

Staring down at your harness, relief washes over you, soothing your tattered nerves. Then both your brass harness buckles simultaneously unsnap. Slowly, you slip out of the harness while clutching desperately at the straps which have become as elusive as quicksilver. Your hands are soaked in a mixture of blood and sweat, making your last gambit for salvation impossible. You scream in horror as the last remnants of hope slither away while the straps slip from your clutched fingers. The cruel wheel of fate has turned yet again.

"Ahhhhh! Son of a bitch! No! No! No! Nooooooo!"

10,000 feet.

5,000 feet.

1,000 feet.

You plummet earthward still screaming, still tumbling, until you finally come to an abrupt, bone shattering stop on top of a patch of desert cactus!

You have just learned what it feels like to be a Police Officer. Welcome to the fraternity.

Chapter Two

The Amazing Spiderman

It was another hot, humidly oppressive summer's evening. I looked at the number on the card in my hand and cursed as I slowly made my way towards the police car lot. My eyes snapped from one cruiser to the next, searching for the one that would be my home for the next eight hours. Suddenly, there it was, staring me down, challenging me, daring me to come closer — to engage.

I grimaced at the thought of what was waiting for me inside the shell of that metallic creature and, although not for the first time, there was no way for my senses to get accustomed to the onslaught that awaited. Beads of sweat formed on my forehead as I took a deep breath, steadied my stance, and pulled the cap off my weapon.

Slowly, I placed my finger on the trigger. My muscles tightened. I was ready to face the beast. With my free hand, I grabbed the door handle and swung it open, simultaneously pressing the trigger on my weapon. The white misty scent of *Lilac Meadows and Rain Forest* shot forth from my can of Fabreze and clashed head on with the lung incapacitating odor of fifteen-year-old, damp, musty, tobacco smoke that sprung from the interior of the cruiser.

My eyes teared as the two battled it out for air superiority, and for a few seconds we had the upper hand, but it was all an illusion. With an irrecoverable blow to my olfactory organ and another to my gut, the now tobacco infused lilac meadows and rain forest scent knocked me back.

"Are you kidding me? Are you freaking kidding me?" I shouted, and tossed the can of Fabreze on the passenger seat. With my hand fanning the air surrounding me, I begrudgingly lowered myself into the driver's seat and shut the door. I peeked at the overflowing ashtray and shoved it shut. The no tobacco policy was implemented over a year ago, but that still didn't deter the cigar chomping, chew spitting, cigarette flickers. Cops are such inconsiderate bastards! Sometimes the dangers of getting into a cruiser can be as harrowing as street patrol. You learn…

The start of the day is not complete without a pilgrimage to the Shrine of Valdez, where a customary offering of silver and copper pieces is made. The servants of the temple will offer you that most sacred of sacreds, the famed *"Nectar of the Gods"* otherwise known to mere mortals as coffee. This devilishly delightful brew is both the savior and vice of police officers, its life-shortening but adrenaline-inducing properties has aided urban warriors since the dawn of its creation. Fair warning, the brew is dangerous to the uninitiated and must be consumed in delicate moderation.

It is often observed that many Police Officers can be seen satisfying themselves with a coffee and donut while on duty. The general public has a strong aversion to seeing what they perceive as their tax payer dollars being wasted. The perception that Police Officers sit around all day scoffing down pastries, slurping dark roast while perking up a dainty pinky finger is hard to dispel. On all accounts, they are right except for one: *"We do not 'slurp' the Sacred Nectar of the Gods, nay we 'sipeth'."*

Leaving the shrine, it was time to get to the tasks at hand. It was a slow night, and that is not a good thing. The hardest thing about being a Police Officer is the long stretches of boredom that often creep in. It was around 2:30 A.M. when the dispatcher radioed me that there was a complaint of a man dressed in a Spiderman costume running around a project complex and acting strangely. This had all the makings of either a prank call or a shit storm. In either case, as a Police Officer, you have to be prepared for both. My first thought was: *"This has got to be a fucking joke, right?"* But since I can't swear on the radio I muffled the f-bomb and started to the location followed by three other units.

We formed a plan of action to break up and search the area in grid-like fashion, but after 30 minutes we turned up nothing, no web slinger. We left only to get a second and third call to the same location. Okay, this was starting to get annoying. Besides, my coffee and Danish were getting cold. I got out of the car and after a quick discussion, we decided to search on foot.

"Over here! I see him over here!" my hand radio crackled to life.

Officer Durge had eyes on the wall-crawler and the foot chase was on. We all started toward the rear of one of the multi-dwellings where Durge headed out with his partner. Just as I rounded the corner of the building, my eyes witness the most improbable and brain searing sight. Staring us down is a man wearing a Spiderman mask and shirt with bright red boots, yet butt naked from the waist down. Officer Durge dove at the fleeing web slinger, missed badly, and tumbled into a nearby garbage can.

"Shit!" he yelled. "Get him!"

Alas, this was much easier said than done as Spidey was proving to be every bit as agile as his namesake.

Officer Griffin was a weight lifter and a health nut, and he was always bragging about some new fad in supplements, which he was quick to try and sell to his fellow officers. I learned a long time ago to steer clear of these types after digesting and then regurgitating one of his healthy concoctions. Either way, Griffin was still in better shape than any of us and as such, stood the best chance of catching the elusive wall crawler.

The moment arrived. Griffin faced off against Spidey, lunging and wrapping his arm around the Marvel hero, wrestling him into a headlock. But somehow, Spidey slipped through the lock. Unfortunately, while Griffin went high, Spidey went low and landed a crushing uppercut that found its mark. A high-pitched scream and guttural gurgling sound followed as Officer Griffin's face contorted into a twisted caricature of pain and anguish. Doubled over and grabbing his low hanging fruit, it was obvious to all but the uninitiated that Griffin was permanently out of commission. It was on…

Seeing Griffin curled up into a fetal position on the ground, Officer Tack stepped in and was next up to bat. This fight was getting seriously humiliating. A half-naked Spiderman, with all the agility and speed of his name's sake, had already disable two of our finest. Officer Tack's metal baton extended with a crisp snap of the wrist as he and Officer Graham closed in on the suspect. Unfortunately, just as Officer Tack swung his baton, the elusive arachnid ducked and avoided the blow. Much to the dismay of Officer Tack, Officer Graham did not. The brunt of the force was absorbed with a resounding crack by Officer Graham's somewhat hawkish beak. This unusual protrusion would forever be bent in a slightly three-degree horizontal angle from that moment forth. Streams of blood spurted like fingers from his now broken nose.

This shit was going sideways fast. Three officers were out of commission, and we were no closer to apprehending this naked, wall-crawling menace than when we started. In fact, we were getting the snot kicked out of us. I was up next and the only thing standing between Spidey and an open field. If he got past me and Officer Swift, we'd never catch him.

"He likes to go low, go low with him," I yelled at Swift as I turned.

The plan was simple, dive middle and low when he was close and tackle him. Woe and behold, it worked! The three of us tumbled to the ground with Spiderman wailing and flailing about like a wounded dog. We crashed to the ground, a tangled furball of arms and legs rolling on the grassy lawn. Lights came on in the windows of the surrounding buildings as curious tenants became aware of the fracas occurring just outside.

"Hold him!" I shouted, as I grabbed an arm and tried to twist it behind his back. I consider myself to be pretty fit. I eat right and exercise regularly, and I knew that I outweighed

Spiderman by at least 70 to 80 pounds. But even so, I couldn't force his arm behind his back. In fact, I was losing control of his arm as he began tossing me around like a chocolate, raggedy Andy doll.

"Hold him! Hold him!" I repeated, but I may as well have said, *ride him cowboy*, because this son of a bitch was stronger than five of us combined. It was then that a thought occurred to me, *does this fool actually have Spidey strength?* I quickly dismissed that crazy notion, but in the back of my mind I found myself wishing for a can of Raid. Officer Swift, seeing that I was losing the battle of strength, somehow managed to cuff one of the mighty arachnid's wrists and together we fought for control for the rest of the suspect's hairy and exposed body.

Suddenly, I felt a strong tug on my holster and my belt spun sideways. To my horror, Spidey had his hand on my weapon and was trying to pry it from its holster. The police department had long ago changed from the standard holster to a safety security holster. These types of holsters are designed to prevent a gun from being forced or drawn straight out, instead requiring the officer to break the weapon forward and then upward. The realization that he was going for my weapon ramped up my response. I rammed my hand over his, holding it there while reaching up and grabbing him by the throat.

I squeezed with everything I had, my fingers digging in and cutting the air flow. There was a long moment where silence prevailed, then Spidey's whole body went rigid followed by a low gurgling sound. Our friendly neighborhood dangler removed his hand from my weapon and clawed at my fingers, now firmly wrapped around his Adam's apple. Fear flashed across his face like a dropping curtain as his Adam's apple was slowly being crushed into apple sauce. Only the weight of fellow officers crashing into us broke my grip. Three more police officers joined the heap and rolled to the ground with us.

IT WAS A PIG PILE! That is, until Spiderman's other wrist was finally cuffed. I lay there in a tangled mass of arms and legs huffing and sweating. The wagon was called for transportation back to the station lockup. The final score was police one, Spiderman four. The suspect was taken to mental health for an examination and was found to have PCP in his blood stream, which accounted for his almost superhuman strength. Although this did not explain his uncanny ability to evade blows, which I chalked up to his Spidey sense. The moral to the story was simple, in the event you ever go hand-to-hand with your friendly neighborhood Spiderman, beware of the sneaky Spidey punch to the twig and berries — check!

Chapter Three

Brawl at the Brass Helmet

Finally, a comfortable spot. In law enforcement it wasn't all work, sometimes days were sprinkled with the occasional oasis of downtime. The frequency of these reprieves, however, was often far and in-between, more the reason to take advantage of any quiet pleasures when you found them. A comfortable spot could be under a bridge, maybe on a side street, or behind a building. The main idea was to find someplace out of the way, the pursuit of which helped put the *peace* in peace officers. On occasion, hiding in plain sight was the order of the day.

If you positioned yourself just right, you could present the illusion that you were working. Mastering the technique of *"Cop Zen"* could fool even the keenest of observers. A citizen passing by would think, "Uh-oh, he's looking for speeders." In reality, you're texting, reading, or even surfing the net. It's what experienced cops are supposed to do when it's slow, and if you've got *common sense.* Unfortunately, I've learned over the years that common sense is not very common to everyone in the police profession.

Some cops listen and learn through observation and instruction, while other wooden *"logger-heads"* just have to stumble and fall upon the hot coals of ignorance. So, it was that at around 01:30 in the morning, Officers Martin and Blake *(against better judgment and common sense)* pursued a suspect into the notorious biker bar known as *The Brass Helmet*. This establishment of ill repute happened to be one of the toughest biker bars in the city. Nightly brawls, stabbings, drug dealing, and inhouse prostitution were the norm. This den of snakes was a dark pit of nefarious activities too numerous to count. The city knew about it but tolerated the activities as long as they stayed contained to the west side and away from the politically elite and well connected. This *"see no evil"* containment method was insurance the vermin stayed put and away from the wealthy. If crime wreaked havoc upon the middle class, so be it, but let even the slightest whiff of the stench of disorder land in la-la land and there'd be hell to pay.

Various biker *independents* (those with loose affiliations with certain biker groups) came to the establishment, but many were enemies. Luckily, The Brass Helmet had a *"truce agreement"* which kept the peace between rival gangs and reinforced the only thing they all had in common: their hatred of the police. Only the mentally insane or deficient entered that place without an army behind them, let alone two officers chasing down a suspect (biker) who was one of their own.

Upon entry, the officers immediately found themselves outnumbered and surrounded. Thus, the dull silence of the early morning hours was broken by a desperate plea of garbled confusion.

"Dispatch! Send us — pzzzzt — help!"

"Jesus! Need — pzzzzt — assistance! Brass Helmet! I — "

Over a chaotic snowstorm of static, the radio fell eerily silent. There was no mistaking that urgent muffled voice or the desperateness of the tone. They needed help, but before I could fully absorb the situation, the radio came to life yet again. This time, a wave of blueberries was calling in from all over the city, many already speeding towards the location of the biker bar. Hastily, I threw my coffee out of the window and floored the gas pedal, or at least that is what I thought I was doing. The cup hit the half-open passenger side window and rebounded, spraying a rainbow of caffeine in my direction with the balance of the hot liquid landing on my lap. Chestnuts roasting on an open fire took on a new meaning for me. The cruiser rocked and swayed as I recited my preschool vowels, "A— Eeee— I— Owww— Uuu— Nuptials! Jeez! Hot! Eeee— Hot! Hot!"

It's amazing just how fast hot liquid can make you move, especially where nuptials are concerned. Making a sloppy attempt to wipe the remaining coffee from my face, I gripped the slippery steering wheel and frantically mopped it with my shirt sleeve. There was no time to curse my misfortune. Slapping a toggle switch on the console, the cruiser's blue lights parted the veil of darkness as I mashed the accelerator to the floor. The engine awoke with a roar and the Crown Victoria surged forward from its grassy knoll like a raging lion. It wasn't long before I arrived at the infamous bar along with a sea of other blueberries.

The single-story biker bar housed some of the toughest, meanest outlaw bikers you'd ever come across. The one thing they had in common was their hatred for any type of authority, especially blueberries. They believed that police represented everything that was wrong with the government and society in general.

Whatever was going on inside, it was sure to be a dangerous furball. I ran to the front of the business where I was met with a loud crash. A blue meteorite was hurled thru a glass window and landed on the sidewalk with a resounding thud. The officer was hurt but managed to stagger to his knees as I ran to his side.

"What the hell is going on? I screamed.

"Ffff—ight," stammered Officer Stanton.

Well, that did it. I turned and entered the doorway

followed by a wave of officers. Proceeding into the dark hallway, I was suddenly stopped by 290 pounds of muscle, a man tree. He stood 6′5 with muscles on top of muscles spilling out of a spiked, leather jacket adorned with various patches. I pressed forward trying to pass. It was then that Mr. Roadblock placed a burly-haired hand against my chest pushing me back.

Now, let me explain. I have a singular rule about touching and my personal space. It goes something like this: *"If you raise your hand to me, you'd better be asking a question."*

It was obvious that Mr. Roadblock required an object lesson on this point. Without a moment's hesitation – which meant I didn't take the time to reflect on the possible outcome – I stepped back and pulled out my canister of pepper spray. Mr. Roadblock's eyes got as big as two dish saucers but it was too late. The orange aerosol mist fanned out striking him in the chest and neck area. I inhaled deeply, holding my breath while drawing my service baton. The effects of the vapor staggered Mr. Roadblock as he clutched at his face and throat. Through watery eyes he reached out for me. I wheeled to the right driving my baton into his thigh. The man-tree wailed like a banshee as he dropped to one knee.

Then, with one hand on his belt and the other at the scruff of his neck, I heaved him out of the front door and proceeded inside the business. There was no time to collect the firewood.

We had to get inside and fast!

Upon entering the bar, I could see three separate battles ensuing, Officer Martin was pressed against a wall to my left. Another officer to my right was pinned to the floor while several rather large bikers were putting the boots to him as he struggled to rise. Officer Blake was on the opposite side of the room desperately trying to fend off three menacing bikers armed with broken beer bottles and a chair. Blueberries spread out in all directions each intent on helping their brother officers.

In the movies, a fight scene is practiced and rehearsed with all the kicks and punches coming in rhythm. The fight goes on for ten to fifteen minutes as the combatants kick the snot out of each other. REAL FIGHTS are totally different. A single punch to the face, kick to the groin, or beer bottle to the head could mean death. There's no, *"Cut! Let's shoot it again,"* and no Queensberry rules. No one, I mean no one, ever shakes your hand after a fight, and you better damn well learn to be keenly aware of that first punch. SA *(situational awareness)* they call it. Learn it as a cop or be crippled. Master it as a cop or die. It's that damned simple.

I moved towards Officer Martin because he was the closest to me, but before I could reach him, I felt steel-like, sinewy arms coil around my neck from behind followed by a vicious tug at my holster! Instinctively, without missing a beat, I drove the butt of my baton backward. The metal found its mark and dug into the ribs of my antagonist. Turning, I drove my baton downward against the hand which encircled my weapon, breaking his grip, and charged the suspect who had unfortunately recovered. My foe grabbed me by the gun belt and collar, flinging me like a chocolate doll up and over the bar. I tumbled over out of control, striking my head on the floor with a loud smack. Flashbulbs went off blurring my vision, a wall of blinding white mist was replaced by momentary darkness. My nostrils filled with the scent of moldy wood and beer, and my back and knees burned with pain. Warm blood started to pool on my tongue which caused me to spit as I violently shook my head trying to clear my vision. Unfortunately, I'd lost sight of my attacker.

Slowly, as I gathered myself, I rose to one knee and looked up just in time to see a chubby knuckled bartender armed with a short, wooden club rushing at me. The bartender had every intention of crushing my skull with the instrument. I rose to meet him, grabbing his arm to prevent the lethal blow. In the struggle, he managed to cram a knee into my left rib cage. Lucky for me, I was wearing a bulletproof vest which I credited with absorbing much of the force of the blow. Off-balance, I instinctively reached back and grabbed a liquor bottle from the bar. In a savage arc, I smashed the bottle against the brute's skull. Blood spurted like a fountain as he crumpled to the floor. Although I still had no time to gather firewood, I could at least secure it. So, I used one of the two pairs of handcuffs I had and secured the subject. With that done, I scrambled to retrieve my baton from the floor and scanned the room for my previous cop launching antagonist to no avail.

In police work we are taught to expect the unexpected and adjust to the situation. Even with that training and years of experience, however, I was ill-prepared for the sight which met my eyes in the ensuing chaos. As I wiped the blood from the corner of my mouth, my eyes were drawn to the end of the bar nearest the exit door. There, sitting alone and without a care in this world, was a blueberry drinking from a frost-rimmed glass. A bottle of Tequila lay half empty in front of him.

The officer sat unmoving, seemingly oblivious to the madness around him. I watched him as he raised the glass to his lips and took a long, slow sip. The pain in my bruised back was immediately replaced by rage. Officers were getting the snot kicked out of them and instead of helping, this idiot who was sitting at the bar having a drink? Are you shitting me? I marched over and slapped the glass out of his hand.

"What the hell are you doing?" I screamed.

No sooner had the words escaped my lips than I noticed a distant and vacant stare in the officer's eyes. His pupils were dilated to pin-points.

The officer did not move or respond in any way. There was blood running down the side of his head from his left ear to his chin, and a long purplish-black bruise destroyed the left side of his face. I grabbed the officer by his arm, opened the nearby side exit, and pushed him outside. I could hear other officers arriving on the scene. Quickly, I motioned to one who was coming to the side entrance and passed off the injured officer. Without saying a word, I turned and went back into the bar.

A hornet's nest of bottles and chairs was flying about the room. I saw three distinct skirmishes and two lesser ones. Officer Reese and another officer were doing battle with what appeared to be no less than five combatants. Judging from their torn uniforms and bloodied appearances they didn't appear to be doing too well. The situation compartmentalized my decision. I had to somehow get to them. Drawing a deep breath, I scrambled to their side. Before I had taken even five steps, strong arms wrapped themselves around my waist and pulled.

The force of the tackle drove me back against a nearby wall knocking me almost senseless. The biker's vicious viselike grip was squeezing my already bruised ribs and it was almost impossible to breathe. Struggle as I might, I was pinned against the wall with barely enough leverage to move. Looking up and beyond the beast who held me all but motionless, I saw another biker approaching fast, his eyes narrowed to slits and a frothy drool of hate dripping from his lips. The biker's intent was clear, for raised high above his head was a heavy wooden chair. I had only seconds to break free. Almost forgotten was the steel baton that I still held in my hand. Viciously, I drove the stick downward striking the rib cage and back of my foe. The blow was just enough to momentarily break his grip and allow me to dodge.

There was a loud, unyielding crunch as the chair splintered, partially embedding itself in the wall. Had I been a fraction of a second slower, my skull would have been crushed. Instinctively, I hammered my fist into the face of the now empty-handed antagonist, driving him back. I turned to my right, bracing my foot to gain the leverage I needed to push off the wall. The force sent my first attacker tumbling backward and over a nearby bar table. He didn't rise (*lucky for me*), and I was finally free, but only for the briefest of moments. A third and even larger biker rushed forward, clamping his hands around my throat. The speed of his attack caught me off guard, and I dropped my baton. Try as I might, I couldn't break his vice-like grip. He was just too damn strong. Slowly, my efforts to break free and the lack of oxygen began sapping my remaining strength. The biker was taller than me by four to five inches, and this made the task of breaking free much more difficult.

STRIKE ONE: I launched an uppercut that landed squarely on his chiseled chin, but this only seemed to make him more determined and his grip tightened.

STRIKE TWO: I punched him as hard as I could in the solar plexus. There was a momentary and forceful exhalation of air, then a redoubling of his effort.

STRIKE THREE would be death, but I sure as hell wasn't onboard with that. I could feel my eyes bulging, and the thumping of my heart kept a deadly rhythm with the ringing in my ears. I felt my legs begin to buckle. As I sagged to one knee, I summoned the last of my strength and launched a palm strike to the biker's groin. To my relief, this did the trick and broke his grip of death. Stumbling backward, I crumpled to the floor gasping for air. My antagonist, yelping like a dog, rolled on the floor grabbing his crown jewels. Before he had a chance to recover, I crawled over to him, placed him in handcuffs, and left him on the floor.

There was no time to claim victory, especially since I hadn't reached my objective. I hastily retrieved my baton from the ground and weighed into the police biker scrum as if standing among a field of corn. I swung my baton left and right in wide sweeping arcs of destruction, striking a knee here, a shoulder there, and anything else in its way. We were tired, bloodied, and battered, but the combined efforts of my fellow blueberries finally drove the bikers back. I could see a second wave of police officers entering the bar and handcuffing everything that wasn't nailed down. In short order, a series of wagons were loaded with bikers and hauled them away. Officer Reese made his way over to me.

"Hey, you okay?" he said with a smirk.

"Yeah, I'm okay… you? Why are you asking?" I was a little puzzled.

Officer Reese looked down at my pants, pointing an incredulous finger at my crotch area. "What did you do, pee your pants?" he chuckled.

Then it hit me, the coffee I'd spilled on my pants earlier made me look like I had wet myself. No matter how I tried to explain it, no one believed my coffee story. The next day, some joker left a small box of potty trainer pampers in front of my locker. There was no mistaking the implication, cops can be some mean, cruel SOBs.

Chapter Four

Flight of the Blue Buzzard

Traffic duty was something you were either born to or not, and I fell into the latter category. So, when Sgt. Lee ordered me to get a few movers on Shrewsbury Street, I cursed him under my breath while employing emotional suppression and visualization.

Early in their careers, cops learned various coping mechanisms and used them with varying success. Mastering this skill meant the difference between career survival or termination. Life in law enforcement was about finding the balance between common sense and insanity, and navigating the social and political minefield wasn't something that was taught in Police Academies. As a new recruit, you watched and learned from others and that was the problem, since you never knew who was the weasel, the brown-noser, the Titanic, or the Unabomber. But one thing that was clear – and understood across the board – it's never a good idea to vocalize anger about an assignment. It was a line that you simply don't cross, and I knew it. You had to self-learn from other cops and quickly.

Sometimes, the advice was sound, but when it wasn't, the whole world would blow up in your face. How did you know the difference? How did you know which scratch ticket to buy? The simple answer was that you didn't. You just pick and hope for the best. The not-so-funny thing about policing was that you never knew anything no matter how much training you got. Basically, you strapped on a gun, pinned on a badge, and hoped for the best.

A police officer always had to know where the lines were, even the invisible ones that weren't found in the rules and regulations, and if you crossed one – even without realizing it – your career was forfeit. One of the hard realities of law enforcement was that it didn't matter how hard you worked or how good you were at the job. What mattered was your connections, how well you were liked, and if you could be trusted not to rock the damn boat.

Police corruption was not a line, but speaking about corruption or informing on others regarding corruption was, and it was the Godfather of all lines. It was bold and fierce, an exclamation point that would get you that horses head in broad daylight, or a shoebox with a dead rat in your car or doorstep. There were rules, blue rules that governed police behavior beyond the regulations. It was part of the Blue Wall that kept police safe from the public and administration and its greatest weapon — silence.

Lying and cheating were a part of it, and anyone who was seen as not playing by the blue rules was dealt with via sanctions. One night, you might be calling for back up that was slow to arrive if at all. It was a clear message of who was in charge and one of many methods to keep you in line as a member of the brotherhood. It was powerful, it worked, and was seldom successfully challenged.

So, instead of anger, I fell back on the tried-and-true method of visualization. I conjured mental images of the sergeant's mother engaged in dubious copulation with a goat. Yeah, it's wrong on many levels, but when looking at Sgt. Lee's scruff of hanging chin hair you'd wonder, too. While a DNA test would possibly set the matter to rest, the thought did help me rationalize my assignment to traffic duty.

In a department with over four hundred and fifty guys, I was the last choice to do traffic duty and everyone knew I hated it! I think I had always hated it. Maybe it was the act of giving someone the hard luck of a ticket. Maybe it was dealing with the ensuing court appeals which seldom ended well, or possibly those tiny, little checkboxes on the ticket that you needed a god damned microscope to see — who the heck was the eyeball sadist who made them tiny checkboxes anyway?

However, orders were orders, so I reluctantly drew a ticket book from the storage box and headed out to the assigned area still cursing under my breath. Shrewsbury Street was in the middle of the city's busiest commercial district. Everyone who was anybody eventually ended up on Shrewsbury Street, especially during the day.

After some fruitless patrolling, I decided to take a stationary position and wait. The air conditioner in my patrol car started to squeak and rattle as if it had swallowed a rat – and maybe it had – because with a loud, gut-wrenching moan it groaned to a halt. I slammed a clenched fist on the dashboard and got a puff of what looked like dust – or more probably rat fur, but the goddamned thing was definitely on the fritz again and dead as a door nail. My tongue was dry and stuck to the roof of my mouth as if I had been munching on dusty Himalayan yak ass, and beads of sweat rolled down my forehead putting Niagara Falls to shame. I opened all the windows hoping for a slight breeze and took a deep breath. All I got was the asphalt's humid, heat-curling version of Mike Tyson's punch to my face. Almost immediately, I felt lightheaded and the world started to twirl. I guess I had a glass jaw when it came to boxing it out with the heat.

I looked down and saw the still closed and almost full cup of Dunkin sitting there, daring me, challenging me – or was it wooing me, I don't know – to take a sip. I was too thirsty to think and my head felt like a balloon, so I didn't argue and picked it up, taking in a big, blistering mouthful.

That's when it happened! Somewhere between my first and second sip of the Nectar of the Gods and the heat induced delirium, I transformed. No longer was I the Peace Officer waiting to serve and protect the citizenry from wrongdoers, nay I had morphed into the crucible of heat and sweat. I sat upon my perch and examined the traffic around me, my focus laser sharp. I was *The Blue Buzzard* seeking my prey, ready to swoop down upon unsuspecting travelers, snatching from them their personal liberties, dignity, and let us not forget, cash! And although the clouds shrouded the sun in a grey cloak, nothing would escape my keen buzzard eyes.

Like the crosshairs of a sniper rifle, my eyes roamed the sea of steel framed beasts until they got a glimpse of my prey, a red Chevy truck rocketing like a metal meteorite down Shrewsbury Street. The area was a posted 30 mph zone and this muff was doing at least 85 mph! The speeder had a good head start, but I was sure that he hadn't noticed me quietly stalking the area and waiting to launch my ambush. I slammed the shifter of my crown Victoria into drive and slammed the gas pedal to the floor, the engine roaring like a caged lion. I heard the tires screech as the wheels spun into action, propelling me forward with a burst of speed while pinning me back into my seat. Reaching down, I slapped the toggle activating the blue lights and siren and focused on the red blur 200 yards ahead of me.

Zigging to the left, then zagging to the right, I weaved my way through the bewildered crazy quilt of motorists. The red rocket was slowly getting closer but still showed no signs of slowing down. The palms of my hands were sweating, making the steering wheel feel like a soggy sandwich. I gripped the radio mike and squeezed the life out of it.

"Dispatcher! I am in pursuit of a red Chevy—"

No sooner had the words escaped my lips than I saw the red rocket veer violently to the right, side-sweep a grey pickup truck, and tear off its door. The vehicle then took a maddening arcing angle and swerved back into traffic.

"Dispatcher, we are Northbound. Suspect vehicle has struck a parked car… requesting backup!"

"Received 63."

I mashed the gas pedal a little harder and the cruiser responded like a wildcat set free, lunging after its prey, almost floating as it careened past businesses and other motorists. The red rocket continued to cut through the traffic like a hot butter knife, heading straight for a red light ahead which might as well have not existed. Without missing a beat, it tore through the intersection as cars with the right of way slammed on their breaks and screeched to a halt while others with slower brake response times crashed into one another. I caught a brief glimpse of a single-car striking a building before bursting into a grey smoke cloud. Still, the red rocket continued. No one seemed injured, and I alerted dispatch to the accidents.

I continued the pursuit, breathing in short spurts as buckets of perspiration rolled down my back. I glanced in the rearview mirror and saw tiny droplets of sweat playing connect a dot on my face. All moisture deserted my lips, and I heard a dull thumping in my ears, while surrounding sounds were barely audible in the sea of the cruiser's siren wail. I glanced at the speedometer and immediately regretted my decision. Nausea bubbled at the back of my throat, and I swallow hard as my mind processed 91 mph down city streets. Fear immediately embraced my senses like a python, constricting, coiling about me. Breathing became laborious. I squeezed the steering wheel and willed myself to focus, trying desperately to clear the mist which had grabbed hold of me.

Clutch butt? That famed malignancy each and every blueberry experiences at some point in their career. Clutch butt was that moment where fear reached levels so great that imminent physiological forces temporarily shut down all restrictive digestive forces. Police Officers experiencing this malady had three probable responses known as Q.S.S:

Q.UIT: Freeze and do nothing. Vacillate in decision making. Run or hide from the danger.

S.HIT: The bodily function that was usually restricted to the bathroom but can occur in policing when faced with a psychologically overwhelming situation. The event was usually followed by a change of underwear.

S.IT: Play it out to the end. Too far into the situation to backoff, so make the sign of the cross, squeeze them ass-cheeks, and keep going.

Squeezing the steering wheel, I willed myself to SIT it out and continue.

"FOCUS! FOCUS!" I mumbled to myself in hushed whispers, trying desperately to clear the mist which lay hold upon my senses.

Luck intervened as the red rocket veered one final time, struck the median, and blew out the front driver-side tire. The tire immediately disintegrated and chunks of rubber sprayed in the air like shrapnel until all that remained was the metal rim. Sparks flew like an amber-colored sparkler as the rim ground and skidded on the asphalt. The red rocket slowed but continued forward swerving wildly left and right.

Suddenly, there was a loud boom followed by burnt, black oil spewing in long trails behind the vehicle. The red rocket – now more like a speeding koala – crawled like a dying animal before coming to a sputtering, grinding halt on the curb. I half expected the driver to bolt from the vehicle, but to my surprise he just sat there staring straight ahead without moving. A trick, or was it resignation to the inevitable?

I heard police sirens wailing, growing louder as they closed in on my position. I offset my cruiser's position from the stopped vehicle in an attempt to create a safe corridor to approach, got out, and slowly snaked my way forward.

The most dangerous part of any traffic encounter was not the pursuit but the stop. The second largest killer of police officers was during traffic stops. The number one killer was going to domestic calls. Every police officer who worked the job knew that fact, and it was always knocking on the backdoor of our minds.

I breathed in deep, and the words *resignation or something else?* echoed in my mind again. He was absolutely still as I slowly approached.

Tha-thump! Tha-thump!

I could feel every heartbeat and rush of blood in my ears. I strained to see what was going on inside the interior of the car, but the glare from the sunlight off the back window was too harsh. Why the hell wasn't the driver moving?

Tha-thump! Tha-thump!

Jesus, I should have waited for backup. What the hell was I thinking?

Tha-thump! Tha-thump!

I couldn't see the driver's hands or if anyone else was in the car. As I took the next step, my hand instinctively moved down to my side and I unsnapped the keeper on my 9mm Glock.

Tha-thump! Tha-thump!

I kept my eyes laser focused on the driver, the palm of my sweaty hand resting on the handle of my gun. Methodically, my fingers pushed the gun retainer strap forward with a click.

Tha-thump! Tha-thump!

My breathing was slower now, deeper. I could feel it reverberating throughout my body. It was like a stone being thrown into a pool of calm water, causing it to ripple out in all directions. The hairs on my arms stood on end and there was a dry leather taste in my mouth. I swallowed hard, but it was as dry as the Mojave Desert. Time slowed to a crawl.

Tha-thump! Tha-thump!

Stupid! Stupid! What the hell was I thinking? I should have waited for backup, but it was too late to turn around. I cautiously took another step forward. My eyes quickly darted to the passenger and back seats as I walked up to the rear of the car. Slowly, without breaking eye contact with the interior of the vehicle, I place a hand on the trunk and press down hard, then gave a slight tug to see if it would open. It didn't and I gave a short sigh of relief. No Jack-in-the-box surprise shooter *this time.*

The driver was like a stone statue, his hands rigidly grabbing hold of the steering wheel. He was staring forward without moving a muscle, trance-like. It was unnerving. Why was he so still? Had I missed something?

There was a black hoodie over his head, and I couldn't make out his features from behind through the closed windows of the red Chevy. Another couple of steps and I finally reached the driver's side door. The smell of burnt rubber filled my nostrils as I tried to suppress my choking reflex. My eyes began to water. Still, no movement. Jesus, WHY THE FUCK ISN'T HE MOVING?

"Sir," I said, my voice low but loud. A part of me — actually, most of me — wanted to scream at the idiot, but I knew that was not the way to go.

No response. Slowly, I inched forward to get a look at the driver's face. He was a scruffy-faced, white male, and approximately twenty-five years old. His eyes seemed distant, glazed over.

"Sir, roll down your window." The command went without any sign of recognition.

"Sir, roll down your window," I repeated, this time a little more forcefully.

The man deliberately turned his head towards me and smirked, his eyes closing into thin slits. I read his body language, his lips pulling downward with a smirk of dismissive disdain. Time seemed to slow to a crawl as we stared at each other for what seemed like an eternity, neither of us moving a muscle. Then, he slowly moved his hand from the wheel and cracked his window open about a quarter of an inch, just enough to let in sound but nothing more.

"Goddammit! What do YOU want?" he barked with such force that a spray of spittle showered the window.

"Sir, I need you to roll down that window and give me your license and registration."

"Nope!"

And with that single-word response, he rolled the window back up. My plan was simple. Get his license, issue the ticket, and wait for backup. But it was clear that this muff was going to make this as difficult as he possibly could. Plans of action were a good way to deal with bad people, but unfortunately not all plans went the way you wanted. I tapped the window with a gloved knuckle and waited for him to look at me. I have a black belt in verbal judo and now was as good a time as any to employ it.

"Sir, if you refuse to give me your license and registration it's an arrestable offense."

Again, that one inch crack of the window. "I don't have to give you shit! I'm a taxpayer. I know my rights!" he snarled. "As a matter of fact, you're a public servant, you work for me! Go get me a glass of water, bitch!" he laughed.

The muff decided to signal me his IQ in the form of a single middle digit then proceeded to roll his window back up. I noticed an ever-widening grin spread across his face like slow-melting cheese. Bitch? If anything, a blue bastard maybe, but bitch? Every cop had a built-in switch, and it had four settings.

SETTING 1: Work it out be diplomatic.

SETTING 2: Difficult person, do it by the book and no breaks.

SETTING 3: Get that son-of-a-bitch!

SETTING 4: Oh, hell no you didn't (in short, my onions were cooking)!

Public servant? Get me a glass of water? Okaaaay… My black belt in verbal judo may as well have been a kite string. This joker was, in every sense, a complete a-hole. Once in a while, a police officer runs into these types and they do their best to shove an umbrella up your butt. Cops don't take kindly to that discomfort, especially when they try to open it. Luckily, I always carry a liberal prescriptive dose of asshole pills for just such occasions. This fine, young scholar was still laughing when my dial snapped to setting four. It was time! I squared off to the car.

STEP 1: Reaching down to my gun belt, I drew out my anti-antagonistic device, which extended with a crisp snap of the wrist. I then wound up like a chocolate Babe Ruth and swung for the fences. The metal baton struck the driver's side window with an ear-splitting *crack*, the force shattering the glass into a million pieces.

STEP 2: A look of absolute horror was plastered across the suspect's face, but it was too late. Without missing a beat or saying a word, chocolate talon-like fingers reached into the vehicle, grabbed this joker by the collar, and extracted his sorry ass through the window. Whirling to the right, I flung the suspect to the asphalt with a satisfying *thud*.

STEP 3: The medicinal healing powers of the shackles of justice were administered to each wrist, each cuff producing a zen-inducing, ratchety click just as my fellow officers arrived on the scene. I wrote the citations and requested a wagon to transport the suspect to the station. While I still don't care much for writing tickets or getting involved with traffic stops as a rule, there are times when being *The Blue Buzzard* has its satisfying moments — Awwwk! Awwwk!

Chapter Five

In-Service Training

The instructors were as straight, rigid, and uncomfortable as the square, back chairs that lined the room. Officers sat with cold, blank faces void of even the slightest spark of enthusiasm. *In-Service Training* was a grueling marathon event, the bane of police officers. I hated being there and hated the long hours of boring speeches that dared you to stay awake even more. But there was no way to escape the ordeal of training since according to state oversight it was mandatory and administered every year. Today's training had only one item of interest to any of us, the introduction of a new department issued weapon, the sleek and sexy 9mm Glock.

Most of the department was still using the outclassed 357 revolvers. The Dirty Harry styled weapon simply failed to meet the harsh realities of changing times. So, it was decided that this newer, more rapid reloading weapon would fill the gap. Unfortunately, the criminals were always trying to get the edge on police officers and had semi-automatic weapons with large capacity magazines. The old "Dirty Harry" revolver held a mere six bullets, had no quick load magazine, and in a firefight it underperformed. The plain, simple truth was that the weapon was antiquated by today's standards. After a few loaded encounters with semi and automatic weapons, our department quickly learned that we needed to move in the same direction as other police departments around the country. That called for changing to a newer, faster reloading weapon with greater range and capacity.

The roar of overlapping conversations died down to a hush when Officer Powell entered the room. All eyes fixated upon the weapon on his hip since most had never seen the 9mm Glock.

"Ok, guys, settle down. I am Officer Powell, and I am going to be familiarizing you with the new 9mm Glock." There was attentive silence in the room, now they were talking a language that we all understood. Guns!

Officer Powell had been in the police department more years than many of us in the room and his professional manner commanded respect both from older and newbie blueberries, so when he spoke it was police gospel.

"Here it is," said Officer Powell as he pulled the weapon from its safety security holster in a smooth, fluid motion that would make Jesse James grin. "This weapon will be replacing the old 357 because we felt that it has a much faster combat reload and is so simple that a child could learn to use it."

Holding the weapon over his head, he continued, "As you can see, it has a 12-round capacity which is far superior to your current 6 rounds, not to mention its quick reload versus your speed-loaders."

There were perceptible ooh's and aah's from the mesmerized officers as the weapon's features were explained. There wasn't a man in that room who didn't want the new weapon, and we were all just itching to get on the range with it and test fire.

Officer Powell carefully removed the magazine and proclaimed, "I want to talk to you about the safety features of the weapon."

It was then that a specific question arose from someone behind and to my right. "Officer Powell?"

"Yes, go ahead. You have a question?" responded Officer Powell.

"Yes. I heard these weapons have a hair trigger. Is that true?"

"No, of course not! These are some of the safest weapons out there. As you can see, you can pull the trigger some distance before—"

Bang! Bang!

Fish eyes! Bulging fish eyes! I didn't understand it, but at that exact moment time froze. My mind flashed back to my first childhood fishing trip. For the first time, I saw a big mouth bass flapping with its bulging fish eyes staring blankly as it was hauled from the water. That lasting portrait was frozen upon the continence of a horrified Officer Powell as the room reverberated with ear-splitting thunder.

Officers dove for cover. One overturned a table while another dove face first to the floor knocking other police officers over like blue, bowling pins. I had to admit, the last time I saw Police Officers move that fast was when it was announced that Dunkin Donuts would be closing early.

The madness did not end there. A tidal wave of stampeding blue rhinos crowded the exits pushing, shoving, and trampling all in their path. I was not immune to the madness having been in the process of taking only my third sip of coffee when the rounds were fired. I quickly found out that hot coffee abruptly diverted into the airway can have a somewhat strangulating effect. I tried to direct my projectile regurgitation to no avail. Spitting Columbian gold, the mixture flew from my mouth in spray-bottle fashion. This sudden expulsion of the hot liquid found its mark on the back and neck of a prone officer.

"Ahh, shit! I've been hit! I've been hit!" he screamed!

"Who was shot?" another officer echoed.

"Someone's shot!" still another yelled.

Unsure of who had been shot, I dove to the floor with the sweet nectar of the gods still dripping from my lips. I looked to my left and right where officers were curled in fetal positions (*reverting to a place of emotional safety no doubt*) as the smell of sulfur smoke filled the small enclosure. Laying there on the cool floor, it only took moments before time resumed and the thunder and chaos were replaced with an eerie silence followed by a snowstorm of white confetti-like particles falling from the ceiling.

Officer Powell stood in the midst of the fine, powdery snowflakes with his mouth hanging open at a crooked angle like a door with a broken hinge. Slowly, his eyes shifted to stare at the weapon still raised over his head. There was a moment of telepathy that was transferred to all in the room. Officer Powell, without making a single sound, mouthed the words WTF! Then, his eyes moved even slower still to the ceiling tiles. There, his worst fears were realized in the form of two symmetrical bullet holes.

"Is... is... everyone alright?" Officer Powell's voice shook with fear. Officers slowly rose from the floor, eyes peering over the horizon of overturned tables and chairs. Relief washed over Officer Powell's face with the realization that no one was injured —except for bumps, bruises, and battered egos. This respite, however, lasted only as long as it took Captain Tolsen to enter the room gun drawn.

"What the hell is going on here?" he roared.

There was a pause as all eyes in the room focused on Officer Powell awaiting his response. The captain, seeing the weapon above Officer Powell's head and the holes in the ceiling, pieced together the events which had transpired.

"You didn't! Tell me you didn't! Powell? Did you? DID YOU JUST —" fumed the captain.

There was nothing that could be said, no ready excuse that would cover this situation. In his haste to demonstrate the abilities of the new weapon, Officer Powell had forgotten the most basic of procedures, activation of the safety switch.

"It was an accident, Sir. I —" he mumbled a word salad of apologies, but the captain was having none of it.

"Accident? Is that what you said? You had an accident? An accident is when you potty in your pants! This is a God damned disaster!" he seethed, snatching the weapon from Powell's hand. "Powell, if your brain were gasoline, you wouldn't have enough fuel to power a maggot motorcycle around a goddamned BB! You stupid idiot! You clumsy motherfucker!" screamed the captain. "Go upstairs and make damned sure you didn't kill anyone on the third floor!"

Officer Power flew from the room realizing for the first time that someone upstairs could have been hit by the stray bullets. I was shocked by the captain's tone and choice words, as was everyone else who had never heard him swear before. The captain stormed off while instructing us to take an early lunch break.

"Hey, you hear the captain call him a motherfucker?" one officer said.

"Yeah, but he's lucky," said another.

"How do you figure that?"

"Well, he could have called him a fatherfucker..."

Chapter Six

Doggy Want a Blueberry

There comes a time in every police officer's life when you had to simply bow to the absurd. When things got so out of control that you knew with complete certainty that there was a higher power at work. I wasn't big on superstition, karma, or religion for that matter, but I did believe that bad things happened to good people. I'd seen and experienced enough of that to know that it was true and that as hard as it can be to accept, it could be funny as hell.

It was 8:45 p.m., steamy hot, and the air conditioner in the cruiser was on the fritz. What made matters worse, I was assigned a partner, Officer Davis, and we were to patrol Route 13. Since we were the only two black police officers working together on that side of the city, we were dubbed *The Soul Patrol* and ordered by the captain to eradicate all crime by 10:00 p.m. — Yeah right!

Like most nights, things were uneventful until we got a particular call concerning a barking dog. As we pulled up to the address, I noticed a lone light coming from a second-floor apartment. I parked the cruiser and we walked up to the multi-dwelling. Officer Davis knocked on the front door, but no one answered. Seeing no obvious side door, we decided to split up and each took a side of the house hoping to find a rear entry door.

Officer Davis was in the department for at least twenty-five years, was smart, experienced, and had been a cop a lot longer than me. Davis was also an avid fitness nut, a runner which kept him in great shape — certainly in better shape than me, although I'd never admit it. The search for the entry door wasn't going well for me, but Davis was having better luck.

"Hey, Charlie, I'm in!" yelled Davis.

"Where you at?" I yelled back.

"It's way in the back on the right. Don't bother, I'm already on the second floor."

Making my way to the front of the house and the cruiser, I decided to wait for Davis. I marveled at just how fast he'd gotten to the second floor since we'd only been apart for a few minutes. I remember thinking, *"Jeez, how fast is this guy? He must have sprinted up the stairs."*

"You find anything?" I shouted.

"Nope, it's quiet. I don't see anything. No dogs around either."

It was a simple thing, a very small thing actually. A slight malignant visual obstruction which is common with old age and infirmity. Exactly what affliction prevented Officer Davis from recognizing the mortal danger he was in, I can only conjecture. But what was certain, was that upon knocking on the door of that seemingly innocent dwelling, Officer Davis had failed to notice the adjoining porch storage closet which housed fifty pounds of four legged muscles and teeth, now inadvertently awoken and angry.

The creature crashed through the wooden door and charged savagely at Officer Davis who in that split moment stepped back, slipped on something wet and slimy, and plummeted backwards down the flight of stairs.

"Ah, shit!" he shrieked, as he rolled and bounced down the stairs like a gun clad blueberry.

The pit bull from hell was in hot pursuit, barking and chomping at the defenseless officer. If only Officer Davis had known just how prophetic his words truly were. Not only had he slipped in doggy pooh, he now found himself being pursued by the architect of his misfortune.

It was while these events were unfolding that my ears perceived a sound so sorrowfully desperate, so filled with trepidation, that it made my blood run cold. Abruptly, the silence was broken by what can only be described as an ultra-sonic, high frequency, bitch scream. Instinctively, I reached down and grasped the reassuring butt of my 9mm Glock.

The hair on my arms stood at attention, charged by some unseen electrical force. Police training automatically took hold, fear suppression, controlled breathing, and hyper-vigilance. All of the tools in a police officer's training and experience kicked in, and I rushed towards the house. My lips were dry, it was hard to swallow, and my heart was doing push-ups against my rib cage.

"Where the hell *is* he?" I muttered.

I ran to the side of the dwelling, stopped, and listened. I wasn't sure what the hell was going on, but the commotion seemed to be coming from the rear of the house. I heard a sound, like something heavy being dropped, and cautiously slid forward with my back pressed against the side of the building. I stopped dead in my tracks at the sight of a screaming Officer Davis, his shirt ripped half off, pants torn, and a face that looked like he'd seen the devil himself. None of this, however, restricted his speedy flight — a blur of blue against the night. At that moment, I could have sworn he was a chocolate Bruce Jenner streaking for Olympic gold. My flashlight beam shot toward the ground, there I saw two glowing, silver orbs and pearly white fangs!

All thought of bravery fled my mental faculties at the sight of that four-legged calamity of impending doggy doom hurtling toward us at terrific speed! The words tumbled from my now quivering lips, scarcely before I realized it.

"Dawg! Big dawg! Big, fucking dawg!" I screamed.

What was any self-respecting guardian of law and order to do when faced with such an ultra-supernatural dilemma? The warrior born would stand his ground and do battle with the beast, while the logical thinker might try diplomatic negotiations. Since I was neither warrior nor diplomat, I chose a more strategic, time-tested approach to the situation. I threw my hands in the air and ran like my afro was on fire! I gained the fence before my partner and sped to the other side of the cruiser, closing the driver's side door behind me.

Clutching my chest and gasping for air I was safe, but not so for Officer Davis. The creature was closing in on him fast. I could only watch in sheer delicious evil as Davis dove headfirst onto the hood of the cruiser, just out of reach of those massive jaws spiked with teeth that could make even the most seasoned officer beg for a desk job. Alas, while I was rooting for Officer Davis, unfortunately, momentum was not. Davis skidded across the hood of the cruiser and as his terrified eyes met mine, time seemed to slow down. In that transparent moment, without vocalizing a single word, I could clearly hear Davis's silent plea. "Help me!"

The four-legged fiend crashed into the wheel well with a

resounding thud. Yet, the beast would not be denied his favorite blueberry snack, complete with a cream-filled chocolate center. Fido scrambled to gain its equilibrium and drunkenly rounded the front of the cruiser just as Officer Davis gained his footing and raced to the driver's side where he frantically clawed at the locked door.

"Open the door! Goddammit! Open the door!" Davis screamed.

Scarcely before the words had been pronounced, the bulky mass of muscled teeth recovered its senses and renewed its pursuit. The beast sought its chocolatey-delicious but elusive prey and would not be denied.

"Run! He's coming around the other side! Run!" I shouted.

"Ah... mother fucker!" Davis blurted.

The creature pursued Officer Davis around the cruiser at least three times. During that man versus beast moment, I had to admire Davis's cornering ability which kept him just ahead of those massive, vice-like, pit bull jaws. Finally, between Davis's cussing and adept bipedal skills, he was able to get into the front passenger seat just ahead of the howling beast. Beads of sweat poured down his face like heavy rain, his eyes bulging from their sockets, his breath short and labored.

"Why didn't you open the goddamned door, you son-of-a-bitch?" Davis screamed.

"Hey man, I wasn't getting bit!" I said, straining to hold back my teary-eyed laughter.

The beast stood outside the cruiser barking and scratching at the door as we released a barrage of appropriate choice words at the animal. Well, that's because we thought we were safe and until Officer Davis took the opportunity to flip fido an indignant middle finger. The creature seemed to take offense to this all-too-human gesture. With froth still dripping from its massive, crooked maw, the creature backed up a few paces then ran headlong slamming into the passenger-side window. Scratching and pawing incessantly, it was intent on getting at Davis.

"Yeah, bitch! I should have tasered your ass!" shouted Davis.

It was by the grace of Saint Michael, patron saint of police officers, that we had managed to escape. But that celebration was cut short by the terrifying realization that fido was backing up again. We were confident that it could not break through a closed window. What we hadn't noticed was another slight, yet malignant visual obstruction common with old age and infirmity and exactly the affliction that prevented Officer Davis and me from realizing that during our travels on this hot summer's night, we'd left the rear passenger window down. This epiphany materialized just as the beast leaped, sailing through the air towards the open window.

Hoping to beat the slobbering quadruped and in perfect synchronization, I rolled up the rear window. It was perfection in motion. We watched in horror as it landed in the cruiser just as the window closed behind it. I had successfully succeeded in trapping the now snarling varmint in the vehicle with us. Thus, for the second time in that remarkable night, not one but two officers belted out ultra-sonic high frequency bitch screams — this time in harmony as we scrambled to escape our self-imposed fight cage.

The creature lunged forward and latched onto my right bicep. Reaching the door handle and pulling it open, I fell from the cruiser like a broken bag of oranges, my leather jacket saving me from what would have been a nasty bite. Shoving the door closed, the evil being was finally contained, although we were now one vehicle down. Luckily, neither Davis nor I suffered any puncture wounds.

Taking inventory of ourselves, we watched as the beast climbed into the front seat of the cruiser and sat triumphantly in the passenger seat while barking and scratching the dashboard. My blood boiled, and I turned to Officer Davis.

"I told you to stop fucking with that dog!"

"Me? You're the idiot who left the window open!" shouted Davis, pointed an incredulous finger at me.

"If I'm the idiot, what does that make you? A shitty-shoe doggy treat?"

For a long moment, we stared at each other, then burst into tearful, uncontrollable laughter.

Animal control had to be called to extract fido from the cruiser using a rite of exorcism, holy water, and I believe a pole lasso. Word spread throughout the department and we were both met with barking noises from our fellow officers. Dog biscuits were left in our mailboxes, all of which made us doggone, howling mad, but sometimes you just have to drink the Kool-Aid and eat the dog biscuit.

Chapter Seven

Verbal Judo

"**I** hate working with rookies! I hate working with rookies! I hate working with rookies!"

I kept mumbling the rhyme over and over again. The plain fact was that no one liked working with them. Being alone gave you a sense of freedom to do whatever you liked without having to worry about offending someone riding with you.

Personality was not in the job description for becoming a police officer. You learn quickly that everyone had their own reasons for coming to the job and not all them honorable. The allure of power and control, the uniform, and money and respectability were all strong inducements to joining the fraternity. Then there were the boot lickers, the booty smooches and suck ups, not to mention those rat-bastard, ass kissers who would do anything to get promoted. These dishonorable sons-of-bitches were the easiest to spot. They came to you with a silvery tongue and asked personal questions about people so they could later use that information against them. There was a mask of pretense, but underneath they were hateful, self-centered, immoral people. These types made up the crazy quilt of police personnel, and thus you learned to guard the gates of your mind.

12:20 P.M.: The police were dispatched to a multi-dwelling regarding a dispute over an alleged stolen bicycle. That seemed simple enough. Stolen bike, quick report, 1-2-3, and we were done. I couldn't have been more wrong. Upon arrival, I met and had a conversation with the alleged victim identified as Mr. Jay Steward.

"Officer, you have to help me," said Mr. Stewart. There was a desperate tone in his voice that puzzled me since it was only a bike, right?

"Officer, a guy named Jose stole my bike and I want to make a police report," Stewart continued.

Police Officers got exposed to humanity at its best and worst, and you heard all kinds of complaints. After a while, you began to develop your 7th sense. We called it the *bullshit meter,* and mine was starting to ring.

"Okay, you say his name is Jose? How do you know his name?" I asked. There was a stutter and all of a sudden Mr. Stewart had a mouthful of marbles and had forgotten how to speak English.

"Well, uh… he and I do know each other, but he stole my

bike and— there he is right now officer!"

Mr. Stewart pointed an indignant finger in the direction of Jose who was walking toward us. We separated the two and I spoke with Jose.

"Jose, Mr. Stewart says that you stole his bike from his back porch, you wanna tell me what's going on?"

Jose looked a little puzzled by this. "I didn't steal anything. He gave me the bike."

"He gave it to you? Why?" I asked.

"He told me if I go over and get him some cocaine, I could have the bike. I told him I'd try."

I could tell by the way he was telling the story that there was probably another explanation to all of this, and I figured Jose just might be going back with us to the station. Of course, that assumption was shot to hell when I spoke to Mr. Stewart.

"Mr. Stewart, Jose says you gave him the bike to go and buy you cocaine. Is that correct?" I say.

"Yes, it is, Officer. But he didn't bring me back the cocaine or the bike. I want him arrested!"

How the heck was Mr. Stewart able to keep a straight face while telling me this story was beyond me. I looked behind him just to make sure he wasn't under alien control or something. When I was satisfied that wasn't the case, an idea occurred to me. This would be the perfect opportunity to train the rookies in problem solving. This call was a furball, typical of the types of calls a police officer got. *Let's see if they can figure it out.*

I asked Mr. Stewart and Jose to wait and radioed a few other training officers to come by with their rookies. The plan was to let them pool their knowledge and see if they could solve this cluster.

Once they arrived, the four rookies got together and I explained the situation and asked them to come up with a solution while we watched. There was a complete look of wonderment as the officers tried to sort out the problem. After about twenty minutes of questions and answers, we asked them what they wanted to do. One officer wanted to stick'em both in the head — nope can't do that, besides there are too many people watching.

Rookie number two and three felt an arrest for the stolen bike was in order until we pointed out that the bike wasn't stolen if it was freely given to Jose. The last rookie admitted finally that he didn't know what to do. Even the training officers were a little perplexed, at which point I finally stepped in with my solution. It did help to have a degree in verbal judo, and over the years I had attained Grandmaster Status.

"Okay, Mr. Stewart, let me see if I got this right. You gave Jose the bike. Is that correct?"

"Yes, Officer, I did," nodded Mr. Stewart.

"And he was supposed to bring you cocaine for the bike. Is that right?"

"Yes..."

"Okay, Mr. Stewart, what we have here is not a criminal matter, rather it's a breach of a *verbal contract* which is a civil matter. The police do not do civil matters. This is something you must petition the small claims court to resolve."

Without another single word or look, we all got into our cruisers and drove off into the sunset. I marked it in my log as a SAS (Silly Ass Shit) incident. Cocaine for a bike, really? You called the police for this SAS?

Chapter Eight

Charge of the Blue Spartans

Stretched muscles crunched and cracked like rubber bands pulled to the breaking point, and your eyes felt like they were filled with wet sand. You rubbed them with the balls of your palm, but no matter how hard you pressed, there was no reprieve. Worse yet, no matter how much water you splashed on your face it did no good. It was the price you paid for working long, hard hours. But you didn't have a choice. Bills were due and despite what the public thought, a cop's salary wasn't worth spit. The real money was working details and overtime when you could get it, but that meant more time away from family. You had no choice, so you sacrificed. Every cop lifted the bar, twin plates of stress and responsibility. It wore on you like sandpaper against your emotions. The pressure made you as hard as a diamond, but it could also bend you towards corruption, or worse — it could mentally break you.

You keep telling yourself that today you won't get hardened, corrupted, or broken. *Lift your weight and keep it up today* you reassure yourself. The clock ticked, but how long could you keep that weight over your head before it crushed you? Five years? Ten? Twenty? Every day, every hour, *tick, tick, boom!* Was today the day you were not that alert and some piece of crap punched your ticket? Perhaps you overlooked that knife or missed that gun in the perp's waistband. But no worries, because you would still get that *special hero cop funeral* with all the dressings — if the brass liked you. Being a cop was always about connections. There were no illusions and not everyone got treated the same in the police family. Some died with every honor we could muster, while others without so much as a kind word. It was a dirty secret we lied to ourselves about, a secret we'd never admit to the public. Most police administration refused to admit that they had a morale problem. If they did, it was the officer's fault and not the responsibility of the administration. When officers retired without giving any notice, it was a tell-tale sign. When chiefs of police hated the players, but not *the game* within their own departments that created them, it was willful incompetence. We all knew it. Good cops didn't turn bad on their own, something had to happen. It was usually *the game* that happened to them, and it was the responsibility of the Chief of Police and all of his staff to put a stop to and crush *the game* and not the player.

You tried not to think about it, pushed it back as you've done so many times before. You closed the door to your mind and pretended it didn't matter when it *really did.* Reassuring yourself, you checked your holster and radio then slammed the locker shut.

"Shake it off, time to go to work," you mumbled out loud.

They said it was normal, but there was nothing normal about the work you did. Hell, you learned over the years that there was nothing normal about the people who did the work either.

Crazy — goddamned crazy was what we all were, chasing people with guns, drugs, knives, and getting spit on by both public and criminals alike. Even in civilian clothes the temperature dropped 40 degrees whenever you entered a room. Nobody wanted to be around a cop, unless they had a bad cop story that they wanted to push on you. All of it was just crazy. The political connections, the everyday, all-day ass kissing, and all of them players in the promotional ladder climbing game. Worms crawling in your gut, but you couldn't puke them out, and it wouldn't help anyway. The worms always came back, as they do — it was the nature of police work. And, *hell no* you didn't know that crap when you took the job. Almost all the baggage that came with the job wasn't advertised and for good reason.

Roll call came and went with the usual fake formality. They called out the cruiser numbers and dealt out assigned patrol areas like playing cards. The sergeants went through the list of names with little concern and questions were best kept till after. Nobody wanted to be there, and everyone frowned on the blue fool who kept them from their ritual coffee or breakfast with dumbass questions. So, you don't ask, they don't tell, and the boat doesn't rock.

Is this the day? The question rolled around in your brain like loose marbles, even as you let your eyes skim over the pile of summons and warrants in the route file folder.

"The lazy bastards!"

You slammed the folder shut, recognizing there were just as many papers in the folder as when you left it two days ago. Officers who picked up the route on your days off were supposed to share the workload and help serve papers, but they seldom did.

The permanent Route Officer was swamped with paperwork, and you cursed the fill-ins who didn't do a damned thing. Fraternity my ass! The Brotherhood? It may as well be the hooded brothers. The police organization was a series of clicks. Those who played *the game* would do anything to get promoted and climb that ladder of perceived success. Lied, planted evidence, sold out their mothers, pimped their daughters... anything and everything. There were no standards, only the ones we hid from the public. The bitter reality was that there were good cops and the *others*. Usually, the others made rank and ran the department. They didn't call it corruption, though. They called it being a team player.

The cruiser started with a roar as you pulled out of the police lot for that first cup of coffee. Hopefully, it would take the edge off. "The day sure as hell didn't start well… at least it can't get any worse," you mumbled to myself.

Almost immediately, your teeth clamped down on your lower lip. "Oh hell, I can't believe that I just said that!" you blurted out loud as if someone was seated next to you. The one thing that you never did as a police officer, you had done. It was the one unforgivable sin, NEVER *EVER* challenge the fates by saying *that things can't get any worse...*

"Car 63."

"Go ahead, dispatch."

"Go to the multi-dwelling to check on the welfare of an elderly man acting strangely."

"Strangely? Do we have the name of the caller?"

"No, it was anonymous. Subject is listed as *use caution.* I'll start back up."

"Received."

And so, it began.

The three-story tenement was unfamiliar as you alight

from your cruiser. Three other cruisers and a supervisor also arrived on the scene making a total of eight blueberries. It was overkill, but there was safety in numbers so you dismissed it and proceeded to the front of the building with the other officers. Once there, you were greeted by the first-floor tenant, Ms. Landers.

"Officers, I'm so glad you're here. You have to do something."

"What's the problem?" Sergeant Ericks says.

"It's that crazy, old man on the third floor. He's nuts! He keeps yelling and swearing at us."

"Swearing? Have you had any problems with him in the past?"

"No, he's just crazy! And there is this horrible smell coming from upstairs. He lives on the third."

"Does he live alone?"

"I think so. He never leaves the house, and he's up all hours. You have to —"

Just then, the third-floor window opened and a white haired, snaggled toothed man stuck his head out.

"You called the police on me? You bitch! Leave me alone. This is my castle! My castle!" he shouted.

No sooner had the echo died than a silver meteor rocketed down narrowly missing Sergeant Ericks.

"Hey, knock that off!" one of the officers yelled while sidestepping the silver toaster.

Unfortunately, this only served to encourage a barrage of objects being cast down upon us like boulders. There were cups, trash baskets, bagels, and condoms. Yes, condoms, one of which landed like a cellophane butterfly on the shoulder of Sergeant Ericks's impeccably pressed and starched uniform.

My great grandpappy Chappy used to tell me how he would stay out and drink with the boys. When my grandma, who was a bible thumping, strait-laced woman, found out about him drinking the devil's brew, she had what Chappy called a conniption. I never knew what the hell a conniption looked like until the exact moment Sergeant Ericks's head began spinning, and a low growling noise emanated from somewhere within that two-hundred-and-twenty-pound frame.

"Get that son-of-a-bitch!" Ericks shouted.

I was the eldest and slowest of the group, so naturally, I brought up the rear. As I passed through the hallway door and paused to look back at my cruiser, that same thought occurred to me again, *It can't get any worse? Can it?*

The journey to the second floor was like climbing Mount Everest. The stairway was exceptionally narrow and pitched at a steep 45-degree angle. Huffing and puffing, I reached the second-floor landing and immediately my eyes started to burn. Snot began running from my nose as I inhaled a lung-full of the nauseating odor of ammonia filled cat urine. The reactions of my fellow officers were similar. Everyone covered their mouths as the stench from the very butt-cheeks of hell was somehow dredged up and fanned about the corridor.

The stench was unbearable and took on the form of a living entity with actual substance accompanying an invisible but tangible taste. Once inhaled, the corrupting flavor rested on your sensitive palette at the very back of the throat, strangulating the uvula. Tears formed in my stinging eyes, and whatever forces that had fueled our honorable accent stalled.

Sergeant Ericks, still angered by the condom butterfly, pushed ahead of us and rallied us forward. Ericks was a true leader in every sense of the word. He never seemed to back down from any situation and wasn't afraid to go into a call with his fellow officers. It was the one trait that set him apart from most officials. His uniform was always starched, shoes shined to an ultra-shine finish, and his pressed creases were so sharp that they could cut a tree in half. Sergeant Ericks was a model of police perfection in every way, and this day would be no different.

The stairwell was steep leading to the third-floor apartment, even more so than the flights before. At the top of the dimly lit stairs was a large wooden door that hung at an odd angle. The hinges were on the right side of the door causing it to open outward into the stairwell. No more than halfway up the stairs, we could hear the old man screaming profanities at both the police and the caller.

"This is my castle! Nobody is gonna get in here. Man the walls!" he shouted.

That did it, and I knew we were in for a prolonged battle. Sergeant Ericks charged ahead, and just as he reached for the doorknob snaggletooth pushed the door open from the inside striking him in the face and knocking him backwards into the ever-advancing wave of blue Spartans. It was only the narrowness of the stairwell, and the officers rushing behind him that prevented him from careening backwards down the wooden stairs.

"That's what you get, you stupid bastards! Get out of here! Get Out!" Snaggletooth fumed and slammed the door shut again before the officers could regain themselves.

A group of three officers assaulted the door, but found it was as strong as a stone gate, too thick to breach by shoulder or pulling and prying. It was then that I heard it, a sloshing sound? What could it be? Then it happened—

The door opened once again and the mystery of the sloshing was revealed as the old man stood before us naked and holding a black, painter's bucket. The sea of blue Spartans surged forward hoping to gain entry before the gate was closed. Reflecting on that moment and the history of the Spartans' ending, and upon seeing the bucket, I quickly surmised that no good could come of that situation and backed away to the relative safety of the second floor landing. I wasn't a second too early as ruin was heaved upon the Spartans.

Snaggletooth had a plan. The bucket contained a tidal wave of excrement and filth no doubt aged to lethal nostril perfection. Thus, with a mighty heave, brownish hell was unleashed upon the officers. Sergeant Ericks, being in the front, turned in horror but it was too late! The rush of urine and human feces covered him and the other officers within range. It was a true shitstorm as officer slipped, rose, and fell again.

"You crazy son of a bitch!" yelled one officer.

"Get that mother—" yelled another.

Sargent Ericks was in shock and too afraid to speak lest he get any of the liquid in his mouth. The others rushed forward now with renewed anger and urgency as snaggletooth reached for a second bucket and was readying to launch another barrage when he was tackled to the floor.

Sergeant Ericks, seemingly oblivious to the actions of his blue Spartans, turned zombie-like and walked down the stairs. Dripping wet, he walked straight past me without saying a word and right out of the building. Shock and awe? Post Traumatic Syndrome? Whatever the explanation, Sergeant Ericks had had enough of the shitshow and was out of commission.

"Hee hee! How'd you like that, huh?" cackled the old, snaggled-toothed man as he was led away in handcuffs and covered in the vilest human, animal waste imaginable. I hopscotched down the stairs ahead of my fellow officers being careful not to slip on any brown cigars or cucumbers, ew!

The fire department was called to the scene. After setting up a quick, improvised hazmat area, all the officers were made to strip and were unceremoniously hosed down. An older wagon was requested for transport of the prisoner, and this, too, was hosed down at the station after the suspect was transported to mental health for treatment.

As for the leader of the blue Spartans? Sergeant Ericks went home for the day and was not seen for a full two weeks thereafter. My fellow blue Spartans were sent to medical for testing and sent home. And since the call was mine, I was tasked with writing the report while trying not to throw up. I learned two valuable lessons that day:

1. Never challenge WORSE because

2. Shit happens, literally!

Chapter Nine

Blue Casualties

Cops drink to forget, it's how many of us cope with the horror of it all. Rape, murder, molestation. Policing is a societal cesspool, and officers tread the filth trying not to get dirty, then jump into the stormy waters without a lifejacket. Often, we fail that swim test.

It doesn't take long for rookies to lose their puppy dog innocence and realize what the public does not, this is urban warfare and there are acceptable blue casualties.

Officer Kate Mullen pried open her eyes, her face resting awkwardly on the hard kitchen table in the very spot she'd passed out the night before. She slowly sat up, careful not to further aggravate the searing headache that was ready to pounce. She wiped the drool off her cheek with the back of her hand and blinked slowly, focusing on the almost empty bottle in front of her.

"Drmn…" she groaned.

Her throat was burning and irritated as if she'd been eating hot sand. She swallowed hard, trying to dislodge her tongue which clung to the roof of her mouth like Velcro. Sunlight radiated through the kitchen window, the thin spears of white stabbing at her eyes. Pressing her fingertips to her temples, she tried to massage the pounding, jackhammer inside her skull into a tolerable throb. It failed. It always failed.

"Argh…"

Kate crunched her eyelids shut and rubbed a shaky hand across them, desperately trying to clear her vision. She opened them again and looked around. The Felix the Cat clock hanging near the refrigerator slowly came into focus. It was already 9:00 a.m. She was supposed to be at work an hour ago.

"Damn, I'm going to hear it again…" she cursed. Pausing to glare at the tabletop, a battlefield of broken Smirnoff Vodka bottles invaded her senses, a drunken tribute to the confrontations with her past the night before.

It was three years since the divorce. It hadn't been over dramatic or messy, but she'd lost custody of her two kids, Matt and Cody. Kate didn't blame Brian. He had been a faithful husband and a good man, but never a strong one. Her drinking and the nightly arguments had taken their toll and led to the inevitable; a failed marriage. It was what it was, one of the perks of being married to a cop. Brian taking the kids was heartbreaking, but a blessing in disguise and she knew that. They needed a better home environment away from the stress and ugliness of her job. But knowing that didn't dampen the pain in her heart. She missed him, the kids, and the stability it brought into her life.

Sighing deeply, she closed her eyes and shook her head. She needed to push back the memories, lock them up at least for the day. Again, she failed. It was a never-ending and losing battle. The ugliness of the job tapped into another memory, one that haunted her in a never-ending loop. It was an open wound from the past, a broken pain that covered her like a heavy blanket and never healed.

The drinking helped, but a little less with each passing day. And without Brian, Kate was lost, stuck in the memory of that terrified, thirteen-year-old girl curled into a ball, hiding in the closet from the monster who came grabbing, touching, and molesting. It was that violating, yet unmentionable thing she had locked away all these years, burying the feelings that had come back, relentlessly pounding on the door of her emotions, tearing down all the barriers where she felt safe.

It had happened nineteen years ago, and nothing was ever the same after that. Kate's blood ran cold, the old memories always reducing her to that frightened and defenseless child of long ago.

"Never again!" she shouted, slamming her fist on the table. There was silence as her words echoed, then faded into nothingness. Unable to escape, she stumbled uncontrollably into a cracked mirror of fractured memories. Kate despised her own weakness. She had sworn that she would never allow herself to be that cowering, defenseless, twig again. Now, she had to prove it.

Kate's career as a police officer spanned nearly nine years, and she trained harder than any other recruit. She needed it, and took as much as the force would give her. She joined the Swat Team, mastering special weapons and tactics, and honed her skills in hand-to-hand combat to a knife's edge. Still, she never felt good enough, never equal no matter what she did. Paying her dues and going above and beyond was just not good enough. No matter how elite or accomplished, there was a measure that she would not be able to meet.

The simple truth was that policing remained a male dominated profession. There was a big, invisible sign which read: Women Tolerated. However, the sneers and dismissive attitudes of her counterparts fueled her even more, strengthening her resolve to be the best of the best. It was the crucible all female blueberries endured, they had to be tough – tougher than any guy standing to either side of them.

The stress from the job and the constant comparisons to

men gnawed at Kate's nerves. Drinking became a release, at least that's what she told herself at first. A casual drink among fellow officers, just to relieve the stress, until it became a ritual. Choir Practice they called it, an informal drinking session where cops let off steam. Law enforcement is a pressure cooker of stress, throwing back a few drinks helped put the job into prospective. But for Kate, it didn't end there. The drinking with the guys spilled over into drinking at home. It was the only way for her to get away from those crushing feelings and truly unwind and escape.

As she become more and more involved with her job, dealing with unconceivable horrors day in and day out, she came to understand just how overpowering her past could be. What she saw on the job bore into her, flooding her mind with her own memories and feelings of pain and shame. To keep sane, she needed to find some kind of reprieve and alcohol become her only solace. Each drink held the promise of forgetfulness or so she hoped. Kate had seen too much darkness and no matter how hard she trained, no matter how hard she tried, she couldn't stop it. The memories and feelings were stronger than any booze she drank.

Truthfulness? Honor? Integrity? It was all such a load of bullshit! None of it was true. LIES on the reports. LIES on the stand testifying in court. LIES to yourself and your friends about the job you do. LIES, LIES, and more LIES! It stacked up in Kate's mind like dry kindling, threatening to burn away all of her moral outrage, her sensibilities. Only the steady flow of liquor seemed to wash out the filth, to dull her mind to what she had become in the service of law enforcement. Steadying herself as best she could, her legs shaking, she stood. The room spun like a merry-go-round, and she collapsed on the floor in a crying heap, it was all so unfair.

Kate wasn't sure how long she was on the ground, but a strange sound intruded on her thoughts. It was a kind of ringing. Again and again.

"What the hell?" she mumbled as the ringing was replaced by heavy fisted pounding on the door.

Scrambling to her feet, she stumbled into the foyer. There was no mistaking the undercover car in the driveway.

"Alright, alright already! Jesus! Come in it's unlocked."

The door swung open and a familiar but concerned face entered the apartment. Detective Richie Connor had always been there for her, and it was obvious why he was there now.

"What the hell, Kate?" he started, then grinned and continued, "Hmm, I never realized you had such a cute butt under that robe." He let his eyes move down to Kate's backside.

"Go screw yourself Richie. The brass sent you out to find

me?"

"Of course, they did. More like to check on your welfare since you didn't call in."

"Are they pissed off?" asked Kate, already knowing the answer.

"Yep. But I covered for you, said you were on a half-day time due," Richie said, a sheepish half smirk on his face.

"Thanks…"

"I can't keep covering for you Kate, so get a move on, you're supposed to be at work by noon."

"Yeah, yeah… give me a minute," she said, heading back to the living room.

Kate found her denim jeans in a crumpled mess beside the television stand. She picked them up and slid into them, trying to ignore Ritchie's obvious lingering stares. She could hardly be shy around him since they shared everything together including the same bed. Richie knew her better than anyone. She had shared things with him that even Brian didn't know. It wasn't clear why she had done it, only that she felt more comfortable sharing her feelings with Richie than she did with her husband. It's an unwritten rule that goes with the job. When you risk your life with someone on a daily basis, sharing your deepest fears and secrets becomes a must. Why?

Because death is always right around the corner.

But their relationship didn't end well, and she always wondered if it was really anything more than sexual tension that had brought them together. There wasn't much to think about, and Kate convinced herself not to think too much about it. Being partners, having each other's back, and having a relationship was complicated – theirs more than usual. One moment they hated each other and the next they were laughing hysterically at something only they understood. For her, there still were unanswered questions. Was Richie just a friend with benefits, or was it something else they both didn't dare admit? Now was not the time to find out.

It was 12:30 when Kate finally managed to grab the keys to an unmarked from the office and hit the streets before anyone noticed. Getting in the vehicle, she reached for a pair of dark sunglasses, put them on, and turned on the car. The feel of the leather seat and rumble of the engine were a soothing balm, and although her head still felt like she had cotton stuffed in it, she managed to get on the road without running into the brass. That was something to be definitely thankful for. Raising a plastic cup to her lips, she let the hot liquid rush past her tongue. The first sip of coffee was always the perfect start to the day, that is, until the radio crackled to life.

"Delta 7…"

"Go ahead, dispatch."

"Proceed to 324 Vale Avenue for a domestic with 603."

"Received."

Domestics requiring detectives to be on scene usually meant one thing – a dead body. The 603 code confirmed it. The only thing left to determine was whether or not it was natural or a homicide.

Arriving on Vale Avenue, Kate noticed a lonely single story grey house set back off the road and flanked by a narrow row of pine trees stretching some thirty feet high that looked like Sentinels guarding the residence. Directly in front of the house were four cruisers and the evidence recovery truck. Officers were standing in front of the home. Kate pulled in and nodded to two of them that she recognized, Detective Richie Connors and Sgt. Matt Wozniak. She parked the car and got out. The grim look on their faces was an indicator and told her more than she wanted to know. It was bad, real bad. Invisible hands pressed on her shoulders, threatening to crush her. It was a typical response, something she had experienced many times before, but it was police work and part of the job.

The guys in the ghost suits were everywhere like ants on a sugar cube. Evidence recovery was for dark ghoulish souls, the kind who didn't throw up at the horrors that they saw. Day in and day out they came to the scene, recorded the statements, made observations, and took photos. Sometimes, they collected the body parts of victims killed or disposed of in the most heinous ways imaginable. On one particular instance, a heartless mother who could no longer stand her infant child's crying, decided to silence the child by throwing the infant into a wood chipper. It's police work, the kind that was not on the advertisement posters.

Processing a crime scene could take days, weeks, or even months depending on the size and complexity of the scene. Every detail had to be painstakingly examined, and no detail was too small to be collected and processed. The police saw and felt all the dark things, the things that no one was ever meant to see. The trick was to get through their career without the dark getting in them. Most of them don't make it, and others get to their pensions only to find out that the dark caught up with them — PTSD they called it. The highest rate of suicide in the nation was among police officers, and it was not a pretty scene. Their preferred approach was to eat a bullet from their own gun, and clinicians and politicians wondered why. Police officers or anyone who had worked the streets, didn't.

Sgt. Wozniak grabbed a clipboard from his cruiser and began flipping through the pages while adjusting his horned rimmed glasses. "Kate, the Department of Children and Families took the girl to the hospital."

"How old is the child?"

"No more than seven or eight. She'll live, but the mother—" Sgt. Wozniak's voice cracked.

"Do we know what happened?"

"The mom walked in on the boyfriend while he was raping the seven-year-old. During the altercation, the boyfriend beat the mother to death with the business end of a clawhammer. The bedroom is a blood bath, most of it came from the mother," he said, his voice trailing off to a tempered whisper.

Sgt. Ken Wozniak was a rock, physically and emotionally, the person everybody turned to when things got out of control. In a tight spot, he was always the first to go in, no fear or hesitation. There was no one better under pressure. This crime scene, however, was another thing entirely. It hit close to home because he had children not much older than the victim. Empathy was a weak spot in his blue armor. It was funny how people thought cops did not have weak spots, but they did… they all did.

"I got it," Kate nodded, and walked past Wozniak to the entrance of the house.

The entryway led to the main parlor which was sparsely furnished. She continued walking down a short hallway coming to the bedroom area. A child's bloody handprint was smeared on the doorjamb, causing Kate to stop dead in her tracks. *Don't think too hard on it, just get through the steps Kate, one foot after another,* she told herself, swallowing hard. *Breathe...*

It's self-preparation and every cop learned how to do it, a coping mechanism if they wanted to stay sane.

The bedroom was an open wound, and blood was everywhere – on the bed, the headboard, the mirror, and the ceiling. There were overturned chairs, and it appeared that the victim tried to run. Kate looked past the bloody mess, her eyes finding the inevitable. At the foot of the bed, a blonde-haired woman lay face down in a pool of blood. The claw part of a hammer was embedded in the side of her skull at the left temple.

The right side of her face was unrecognizable, her right eye partially dislodged from its socket with the force of the blow. Grayish-pink brain matter oozed from her nostrils. The spaghetti like flesh extended to her right cheek, disappearing behind her ear. Her right arm and wrist were broken, like the awkward angles of a marionette puppet whose strings were cut.

Kate took a deep breath and exhaled. This one had fought for her life. This broken puppet fought hard and lost.

Kate turned her head from the bloody scene and gulped air. She needed to suppress the queasy feeling in the pit of her stomach before contaminating the area with her breakfast. Swallowing hard, she tasted the coffee from earlier rise to her throat.

Officer Marty from evidence recovery entered the room and walked over to her.

"Marty, where was the daughter found?"

Marty frowned and pointed at the closet.

Kate walked to the closet and opened the door. "Jesus! the mother must have hidden here," she said, staring at a massive pool of blood on the floor.

Marty shook his head. "No… that's what we thought at first, too." The veteran officer's eyes teared up, and his words came in a low, guttural baritone. "He raped her then put her in the closet. The blood belongs to the girl. I never knew a little girl could bleed so much," he said, his voice trailing off into silence.

Kate averted her eyes and squeezed them shut, pushing the nauseating emotional vomit to the back of your throat. Police officers learned to flip the switch, empathy on, empathy off, it was the only way to make it through the work day. Those who didn't were the ones who ended up crossing the line. They beat on people, killed someone, started to drink and drug, or just plain went nuts. It was the job, the part people didn't want to talk about or denied even existed. Cops were supposed to always be strong but never human, never... human.

Kate took another deep breath, composed herself, and pushed past Officer Marty exiting the room. Detective Richie was standing in the adjoining hallway.

"Kate, you alright?" Richie's voice was low and whispered.

"Yeah, I'll be alright. Just a little too much blood is all," she lied.

Ritchie looked at her, his eyes searching hers. He knew. Before he could respond, Kate bolted out the front door. There was no more to be learned. She had the what and needed to discover the why? Her personal issues were not pertinent.

Turning the key, the Crown Victoria's engine roared to life. Thinking about the blood and the little girl, Kate put the gear into reverse and floored the accelerator. The vehicle bolted back, sending dirt and gravel flying. She screeched to a halt in the street, jammed the gear into drive, and sped off mashing the accelerator much harder than necessary.

She needed air, something to clear her mind. Rolling

down the window, the frigid autumn air stung her face and eyes. The fingers on both hands were numb as she gripped the steering wheel too hard.

Everything was spinning, and the pit of her stomach was in knots. The voices in Kate's head were screaming again, a mash of what she had just witnessed and the childhood nightmares she was so desperately trying to leave behind. She urgently needed to put space between herself, the house, and— that closet.

As the house faded in the rear-view mirror, she slammed her fists on the steering wheel unable to check the flood of anger and anguish. Tears welled up in her eyes and she wiped them on her coat sleeve. Almost as if it was a stranger's hand, she watched as it slapped the latch that opened the glove compartment. Reaching into the small, cluttered area she pulled out a bottle. Breaking the seal, Kate hoisted the bottle to her lips, allowing the clear liquid to pour in, drinking deeply.

It was a full hour before her nerves settled down. But something was different now. For the first time in months, her mind was clear. Pulling into the familiar parking spot, she knew the suspect was processed by now. It was time to get some answers.

Kate stepped out of the car and walked to the building.

Unnoticed, was the slight smirk on her face. Unnoticed, was her purposeful and determined walk. Unnoticed, were her fingers tightening around a concealed 38 revolver.

"Breathe… just breathe," she said under her breath as she entered Police Headquarters.

There was a decision to be made, the choice of twins, that *thin blue line* that cops straddled every day — the line between light and dark, justice and revenge. A voice echoed in her head, *What will be your choice?*

Kate didn't know. The only thing that mattered was the answer to questions from long ago. The perp knew the answer, he knew it when he crushed the skull of the mother with that clawhammer. He knew it while raping that innocent little girl, twisting her mind and spirit into a shattered husk. He broke that twig.

Kate entered the elevator, bit her lower lip, and punched the 6th floor button. The interrogation consumed her thoughts. She was determined to make him answer no matter the cost. Today, she was going to find out, to finally be free.

Squeezing the butt of her revolver even tighter, she made a decision: *this asshole will never break another twig.*

A bell rang and the heavy, metal doors slid open. The elevator had reached its destination. She stepped out into the brightly lit corridor. A lone figure, his face an image of concern, stood there looking at her.

"What are you doing here? I thought you were still at the crime scene," said Kate.

"I was… then I went to the hospital to see the girl— she didn't make it," said Ritchie, his eyes averting Kate's. "I wanted to be here for the interrogation, you gonna be okay with this, Kate?"

"I don't need you to hold my hand, Richie. If that's what you mean."

"Yeah, nothing hurts you, right? Always the indestructible one, the invincible Kate Mullen. The brass cupcake."

"What the fuck is *that* supposed to mean? You're the one who couldn't commit, who walked out! No, ran out on me, remember?"

"You know that's not why I— forget it." Richie's voice dulled to a whisper as the elevator doors opened to a corridor of people.

There it was again, the one thing about Richie that Kate admired most. He knew where the emotional lines were, the ones that shouldn't be crossed. He knew when to let things go. Brian was nothing like that, the bastard held on to an argument like a dog's chew toy. That just may have been the reason, that one thing that made Kate fall for him.

The Detective's office was a cluttered mess of ten work desks crammed together in the barely adequate enclosure. Upon each rested stacks of case folders, some to be worked on, others closed out. The sight seemed overwhelming, when in fact the opposite was true.

"Hey," said Richie, as he nudged Kate in the ribs with his elbow and nodded in Captain Roy Campbell's direction.

The captain looked back, his face grim. "Kate, the perp is in the interview room. He's been sitting a while to let him stew," he started. "We've been working him since he came in, but he's a tough son-of-a-bitch. Keeps quiet," said Captain Roy, throwing a stack of papers on the desk.

"I'd like a crack at him, Captain." Connor's voice was eager.

"Wait a minute, this is my investigation. I'm doing the interrogation—"

"You both are," interrupted the captain. "Kate, you take the lead, Richie you're the second on this. You'll only have a little time with him, his lawyer is already on the way. Get as much as you can in the time that you got understand?"

They nodded in agreement.

It sat sullen, motionless, soundless, a smoldering amber in the small enclosure. Silvery eyes resembling that of an Alaskan husky lay partially covered by a wisp of oily black hair. The dull gaze of the man was transfixed upon an invisible spot on the wall, and his breath came in short exhales barely moving his large muscular frame. There was the smell of crazy all over him, something restrained like a balloon full of water almost at the breaking point. The unsuspecting would see him an invalid. Yet, to the trained eye, there was perceivable tremor. *It* moved — it swayed back and forth in rhythmic cadence to a soundless harmonic. The movement resembled that of swaying leaf ensnared in some unfelt invisible breeze.

At the rooms center and positioned slightly to the right of the entrance, a drab steel table and bench was bolted to the floor. A single metal chair oasis was purposefully positioned in the corner. The enclosure was a blank slate of lifeless décor. This, too, had its purpose. No clock, no exterior windows, no distractions. The large, metal framed steel door was the only entrance or exit, it was a cell for all intents and purposes.

Jacob Little wasn't afraid of the police or what fate might befall him. Incarceration was nothing new to him, and the road to prison held no surprises. He had given up on fear and hope. When he was thirteen, he had left home fleeing a sexually abusive father and absent mother. No one cared, and the ones who did quickly fell away abandoning him.

It was a cycle that never seemed to end. Some days, he would punch the walls screaming until his lungs ached and his knuckles bled. The drugs helped dull the bad memories, but like a rushing river, the demons of his past would come back, haunting him even in his waking hours. No one helped, no one understood, how could they? A hatred burned within him and no matter how hard he tried, he couldn't control it, he just couldn't.

Kate and Ritchie entered the interrogation room, closing the door with a loud bang. The stage was set and they had to be in control. Kate looked at Jacob, then pulled the steel chair from its corner, the metal legs screeching in protest as she dragged it to the table. She sat down in front of Jacob and placed a steno pad on the table, crossing her arms. She was staring at the *it* from her past.

A checkerboard of scars was visible on both forearms, the kind that only self-mutilation can explain. Along the suspects right cheek was a long scar winding its path along his square jawline and ending at the base of his ear. It was obvious that its author meant only to disfigure and not kill.

Be calm... wait... It was years of training and instinct guiding Kate now. The pause was essential, a purposeful moment when an interviewer sought dominance over the interviewee. It was a game of mental chess.

Jacob slowly lifted his head as gravity pulled the corners of his mouth into a fiendish frown. "What do you want, bitch? I ain't saying shit." His voice was a low, guttural growl meant to intimidate.

"I've come to talk to you, Mr. Littleton, about what happened," said Kate, straining out any emotion in her voice. The game of chess had begun.

"You want to know why I did it? You want me to tell you, is that right?"

"Yes, why did you?"

Jacob leaned forward slightly, his eyes mere slits. "Okay, here's why…" he said, and spat in Kate's face. Leaning back, he roared with laughter, the noise filling the room. "How's that for an answer, bitch!"

Richie had seen enough. Launching himself forward, he grabbed Jacob by the throat in a vice-like grip. A stifled gurgle replaced the laughter, and Jacob's face contorted into a mosaic of writhing pain as talon-like fingers constricted his windpipe. "You find this amusing, asshole?"

"Hey!" Kate shouted, jumping from her chair and grabbing Ritchie's arms, "Let him go!" Struggling for a moment, she finally pried Ritchie away.

Wiping the spittle from her face, Kate looked down at

Jacob, her eyes cold. "Enough of this shit," she hissed. "Why did you rape that little girl? *Why?*"

Jacob stared from one to the other, the silence heavy. It was the moment before the scare, before the bomb dropped.

"You two are really touchy. Okay, I'll give you what you want to hear... the details," Jacob grinned. "The girl, she was so tender. Hell, her mother never really paid her any attention, cause she never had any attention for herself... you know the type. They grew up all fat and ugly, the girl nobody wanted to date, no one wanted to even be around, the jokes and stares. The obese punching bag everybody just had to take a whack at. Women like that, you just have to give them a couple of kind words and bingo, straight in the sack. I was never interested in that fat slob, the mother didn't mean shit to me, just the daughter."

"How did you know she had a daughter?" Kate asked, her voice flat.

"That was the easy part. I'd wait near the playgrounds, sometimes at the school bus pickup spots. I'd see the mother come to pick her up, it was easy enough to follow her home and learn the routine."

"How long did you watch her?"

"I don't know, a few weeks— STOP FUCKING

INTERRUPTING ME! Do you want me to tell the goddamned story or not? Then, shut the fuck UP!" Jacob seethed.

It took a deep breath, calmed himself, and started again as if nothing had happened. "Sometimes, I would watch her playing in the schoolyard. She had such soft skin, so smooth." Slowly, Jacob shifted in his seat and turned to face Kate. "She had eyes like yours, you know, skin like yours. I watched her, the way her little body moved, and I knew. I knew I had to have her. She was mine. So, I pretended to be interested in the mother, to gain her confidence. If I could get close to her child, in time— the silly cow never even suspected. She actually thought I loved her as if I could love something like that."

Kate clenched her jaw as images started to materialize in her mind's eye as they had done so many times before. Her face flattened to a distant stare, sweat beaded up on her face and forehead, and her throat constricted to a point that it was hard to breathe. Past memories flooded Kate's senses as rough hands grabbed her, caressing her soft skin. Suddenly, a heavy hand clamped down over her mouth and nose muffling her screams. There was a heavy, immovable weight pressing on her body, the smell of a familiar aftershave mixed with alcohol. *It* is taking her.

Jacob continued his tale as both Kate and Richie stepped

back from the table. A strange look spread over Richie's face, his eyes crunching into thin slits. Kate looked at him, recognizing the expression, but not sure from where.

"That stupid bitch finally left me alone with her. She was playing in her room, and I knew it was time for me to teach her how to be a woman. I—"

Kate's scarred mind shut out the rest, pulling out a 38 revolver. With trembling hands, she aimed the weapon at the monster from her past, leveling it on *it*. The memories crashed into her in waves of nausea. The endless beatings and punches that came from the hands that should have been protectors. Getting struck and whipped with extension cords, lashing and scarring her young body on the back, legs, and neck. Forceful hands holding her down in a tub of scalding hot water. The bath filled with the choking smell of Clorox bleach. There was nowhere to run, no one to call to for help. She was a twig, a useless twig that nobody noticed or wanted.

There were the badges, the swollen lips and nose, the bloodied mouth, and the blackened eyes that could not be explained by slips and falls. So, Kate withdrew into herself and pretended that she was anywhere except where she actually was. It was an escape, if only in her own mind. The indignity and shame of wetting her bed, the confusion at not knowing why? The neglect of her mother's so-called boyfriends who treated her as their own, personal sex toy. A mother so consumed with her own pain, guilt, and alcohol abuse to notice.

Jacob, the *it,* had keys that unlocked the doors to Kate's past. It all poured out in an uncontrollable torrent of rage, fear, shame, and revenge.

Then came a high-pitched voice that reverberated throughout the room. "You shouldn't have done that to me! You shouldn't have!" A scream that was repeated over and over again.

Suddenly, a single shot rang out, the noise almost deafening in the small room, it's accuracy deadly. Jacob was thrown backward, the impact knocking him from his chair. A cloud of smoke and the smell of sulfur filled the room as he lay motionless on the ground in a pool of blood.

Tears welled up in Kate's eyes as she looked down the barrel of her gun. It was finally over.

Several detectives, including Captain Campbell burst into the room and grab Kate.

"Noooooo!" screamed a voice.

Slowly, Kate turned to Ritchie who was on his knees, his revolver still smoldering in his hand.

"Richie why? Why?"

"Kate, I... I had to, don't you see? It was me. You understand? It... *it* happened to me," he said in a trembling voice, tears running down his face.

The long years of pretense were finally over. *It* was finally over.

Kate staggered back into the corner of the room, still unaware of the revolver in her own hand. Dropping her gun, she crumpled into a ball of tears, grabbing her knees, and pulling them tightly to her chest. *Richie? He was just like me... why couldn't— why didn't I see it?*

Kate pulled her knees even tighter to her chest and started to rock slowly back and forth trying but failing to process the pain, the realization — that Ritchie was just like her, a broken twig.

Author's Note*

Too often police officers are thought to have no emotions, no empathy. Police Officers who experience the horrors of the job over years of service can and do develop PTSD. The pressures and demands of being a police officer have grown more severe and, for the most part, PTSD goes undiagnosed. Stress councilors and departments presuppose that officers will seek help on their own, but they are wrong. Most officers don't even know the symptomology. It's not taught in the academy and it should be.

It has been my experience that police officers often don't realize they have a problem even when it reveals itself on the job. The administration turns a blind eye refusing to admit the problem exists in their departments. Currently, in Massachusetts, there are no programs to specifically deal with the detection of PTSD in police officers. Stress is nothing new to the profession, but there is confusion. Stress in general and PTSD are NOT one and the same. Each should be managed and treated differently.

The Massachusetts State Police, Boston Police Department, Worcester Police, and Springfield Police Departments, at the time of the writing of this book, have not addressed this *specific* issue. It is hoped that with awareness of the problem, this will change. We don't need any more Blue Casualties. I want to especially thank those officers for being candid in relating their personal stories. May Saint Michael always protect you and your family.

*Additional Note: The suspect in this story, although shot, did not die. He is currently serving life in prison with no possibility of parole. Both officers in this story have been retired with stress-disability pensions and are currently receiving mental health support.

Chapter Ten

Circle of Life

Officer Jason Todd arrived at the local Audubon Society Wildlife Sanctuary much to the delight of the mass of elementary school children. There were no less than four full school buses.

"Officer Todd! Officer Todd!" the children shouted in a chorus of greetings which made him blush.

Officer Todd believed in building community relationships, and the children genuinely enjoyed his visits, especially when he brought different animals for them to look at. A certain freckled faced, red-haired girl struggled to see the officer. Amber Lynn had formed a fond, big brother attachment to the gruff, gravel voiced police officer. She'd found it difficult to open herself up to anyone, but when the salt and pepper-haired Officer Todd started coming to her school, she befriended him and the animals he brought.

Teachers and therapists noticed the connection right away, even when Officer Todd did not. Amber came from a very poor family, and not long after her birth her father passed away from a heart attack. Her mother tried to love little

Amber, but the grief over the loss of her husband left no room for the little girl. Time passed. Soon, despair sought refuge in alcohol and the promise of forgetfulness.

The cycle of an alcoholic morphed into self-isolation and neglect. Amber was reduced to an excuse, a painful reminder of the shattered life that was no more. Her mother slowly withdrew from the world and Amber. The shy, tiny framed red-haired girl needed someone, anyone to make her feel safe and loved. It was an odd, unlikely replacement for sure, but for now, Amber's blue security blanket would be Officer Todd.

The school children unloaded from the busses, and the teachers marched them to their destination with drill sergeant-like efficiency. A few minutes later, the children all sat in the large common area of the building and Officer Todd found himself addressing the group. The gossiping murmur of the children stopped almost immediately as the officer began speaking.

"Okay, children, settle down," said Officer Todd. "As you can see, I've brought a few friends to show you today. Now, if we can all be very quiet so as not to scare the animals, we can begin."

The teachers directed the children to move closer and form a semi-circle around Officer Todd, which they did with all the organization of worker ants. All eyes focused intently on the cages which were placed on nearby tables just to the right and behind the seasoned officer. Officer Todd removed the covers to reveal several of his friends.

There was a baby fox, a large snake, a large shelled turtle, and a mystery cage which the officer did not immediately reveal to the children. This special cage sat apart from all the others and remained covered. One child raised his hand.

"Officer Todd, what animal is under that sheet?" the little boy asked, pointing to the single cage that had not been revealed.

"That is my special animal. Today, we are all going to release it into the habitat. You're all going to get to see me do an actual animal release."

The children went wild with excitement, so much so that all during the lecture, questions kept circling back to the covered cage. It was clear to Officer Todd that the covered animal had completely taken center stage in his presentation.

Forty minutes came and went until the moment had finally arrived. The Audubon Society had a fenced in habitat area which contained all sorts of wildlife. The land had been left to the society long ago as a preserve. The main building's rear deck overlooked an area that offered spectators a keen vantage point to observe the rolling hills, forest marshes, and many animals that inhabited the preserve.

The teachers, at the direction of Officer Todd, swung into action. The mass of children was herded onto the large deck's open area just outside the gathering room. This area was more like an outdoor lounging area where visitors could stand outside and see the adjacent forestland. It was the perfect spot from which to do the release, thought Officer Todd.

"Okay, children, here is the animal we are going to release."

Officer Todd then lifted the sheet to reveal a small white and grey pigeon.

"Ooooo," sighed the children in unison at the sight of the tiny creature.

Little Amber was transfixed by the small creature. It reminded her of someone. It seemed so helpless, defenseless, and fragile — somewhat like her.

"I need everyone to be very still," said Office Todd. "When I open the cage, the bird will come out and fly off into the habitat, but only if we are all very quiet."

The Officer made his way to the cage and opened the latch to the crate. Slowly, he pushed the gate wide then stepped back and waited. Every eye focused on the bird which paced back and forth within the cage. The teachers, the children, and the workers at the arboretum all watched — and watched — and watched. A mass of humanity each holding their collective breaths. The moment was consuming, no one dared divert their attention from the event. Agonizing seconds stretched into minutes of inactivity which seemed to last forever. Nothing was happening.

Officer Todd and the children were getting impatient with the bird's refusal to take flight. Suddenly, the pigeon came to the edge of the open cage and timidly peered around both sides of the opening. This was the anticipated moment they were all waiting for. The bird would surely take flight and settle on one of the nearby trees. This hope, however, was dashed by the apparent squeamishness of the creature. It quickly darted back inside the cage and refused to come out. It was evident that the bird was unwilling to cooperate, something had to be done.

Hastily, Officer Todd devised a plan. He would entice the bird to leave with a bread-crumb trail. Officer Todd placed a couple of the morsels just outside the cage and it worked! The pigeon slowly ventured outside the cage, ate the small offerings, then quickly returned to the cage.

What the heck is wrong with this dumb bird? thought Officer Todd. The children and teachers were beginning to lose interest when the officer had another idea.

Officer Todd, with the help of Amber Lynn, would lay a

longer bread trail leading the bird further away from the cage. The shy creature would have no choice but to come out. Once far enough from the safety of the cage, it would most likely take flight. The plan was set Officer Todd and Amber Lynn was more than eager to help. She placed the bread crumbs down just outside and away from the cage and they all waited.

"Officer Todd," she said, looking up at the officer.

"Yes?"

"Will the dird come out and fly away?"

"I sure hope so. These crumbs should help," said Officer Todd.

The plain truth was that Officer Todd couldn't really be certain what would happen. After laying down the trail of crumbs, he and Amber Lynn went back to the group of children and teachers and waited. Soon, their hard work seemed to pay off. Within moments, the little bird left the relative safety of the cage and started eating crumbs, then took a few steps forward and ate more. Slowly, it made its way down the breadcrumb trial.

Triumphantly, Officer Todd looked back at the children, a satisfying smile of victory crossing his face. Slowly, Officer Todd pulled on a piece of twine which he had attached to the cage door. The gate swung shut, effectively barring the creature's return. Officer Todd turned toward the children and stated: "Now, children, if you watch very carefully, we will see the bird take off and fly away."

No sooner had Officer Todd spoken than there came a loud screeching noise from above. Unknown to all, keen and sinister eyes peered greedily upon them from on high. There came yet another screech that caused the children and teachers to suddenly recoil. All heads turned skyward as a large, black shadow appeared seemingly out of nowhere. The shadow grew larger and larger and slowly took form as another, final wail fell upon the ears of the children.

The children, many of whom stood frozen, placed their hands over their ears in fear. Officer Todd had spent many years training in the wild. He knew what was sure to follow and his heart sank. The pigeon looked up and realizing the danger, instinctively flew toward the cage for safety. The dark shadow grew larger still and completely covered the form of the small bird.

In a fearful frenzy, the pigeon flew directly into the now closed cage just as the hawk swooped down raking feathers from the pigeon. The cage offered little protection from the attack. The children shrieked and began running in all directions!

"Ms. Jones, don't let it eat me! Save me! Save me!"

shrieked a little boy.

A chorus of terrified voices echoed from the mass of children. Those too frightened to move stood as rigid as cement pillars, eyes transfixed as the struggle of life and death unfolded before their very eyes.

Amber Lynn had already fled towards the relative safety of a nearby teacher. Officer Todd tried to compose himself as he watched tiny arms clutching the legs of the educators. Amber's tears streaked her face like a dirty storefront window.

The little bird was down, momentarily knocked senseless by the sudden attack of the large hawk. It darted from the ground again in a desperate gambit to preserve its life. Unfortunately, the crumbs it had eaten slowed its otherwise speedy flight. The large predator would not be denied its prey and large, razor-sharp talons extended and grasped the small bird in mid-flight.

Again, there was an ear-piercing shriek, but this time it was not of the hawk's making. Sixty, four, and one. Those numbers would be forever seared into Officer Todd's mind, for that was the number minus one of those screaming voices. Sixty screaming and crying children, four terrified and screaming teachers, and one lone animal control officer who watched. Sixty, four, and one.

What followed next was a sight never meant to be seen.

Yet, as much as Officer Todd wished it, it could not be unseen by the children and teachers present. A most bloody scene met the horror-stricken eyes of the children. The hawk, eager to feast on its prey, landed on the ground mere feet from the children. There, with prey under talon, it pecked savagely at the still flapping bird.

Children screamed as a new wave of fear invaded their senses. The sight of bloody gore and bird entrails flopping about the ground and the hawk feasting upon its still quivering prey was too much to bear. The children shrieked anew with each new mouthful of flesh the hawk ripped from its victim. Again and again, the hawk plunged a bloodied beak into the lifeless carcass.

The blood-stained bird feathers resembled an exploded party favor. Feathers from the kill drifted toward the screaming and crying children. Soon an avalanche of chaos gripped the hoard of children sending them stampeding into the arboretum.

Teachers rushed in to stem the tidal wave of fear. It was too late! There was wailing and gnashing of teeth! Terrified first and second graders running in all directions seeking some safe haven from the killer hawk.

"Run!" "Run!" someone shouted.

"Don't let it eat me!" screamed another!

Toddler Armageddon had broken loose and there was no containing it. Officer Todd did his best to direct the children inside. Finally, he was able to scare away the hawk which flew to a nearby tree still clutching its prey.

All the children were gathered inside the arboretum and went through a lengthy headcount. Many refused to be calmed and wanted to leave that very moment. But what of little Amber Lynn? Officer Todd searched and could not find the redheaded girl until there came a tap on the officer's shoulder from a teacher.

"Officer, is the hawk gone?"

"Yes, I think I scared it away," said Officer Todd.

Then, there came a tug upon his pants leg. Looking down, the officer noticed the red hair and puffy, bloodshot eyes of Amber Lynn looking up at him. As Officer Todd bent low, Amber Lynn's arms encircled his neck and squeezed with all the strength she could muster. For a long moment, she held on tight before finally letting go and stepping back.

"Officer Todd," she said.

"Yes, honey?" Officer Todd replied. He could not help but noticed the little girls folded arms and stern penetrating stare.

"You killed the dird!" Amber's eyebrows scrunched together and her bottom lip pulled down like a window shade.

Officer Todd would never forget those words, or the small balled up fist which struck him in the chest. Amber Lynn was led away by her consoling second-grade teacher. Despair intruded upon the jumbled thoughts of the salt and pepper haired officer. Perhaps, it was the mosaic of splattered bird entrails or the remembrance of the terrified faces of that stampede of fleeing youthful humanity.

Officer Todd fought hard but failed to stop the single tear which rolled down the side of his cheek. Taking in a deep gulp of air, his palm swiped the moisture from his face. Gripping the steering wheel, squeezing it tightly, he reluctantly turned the key to his cruiser. Sadness constricted his throat. The facts were undeniable, and he knew he was convicted.

Amber Lynn had judged correctly, *he had, indeed, killed the dird...*

Chapter Eleven

Home on the Range

Officer Stephen Gant sat on the hard wooden bench staring at his locker through a haze of bloodshot eyes. The nasal assault of coffee beans, stale beer, and feet swirled about the locker room. It was too damned familiar, too comfortable. Gant rose to his feet and began to fall forward before clutching the locker door, his knees buckled slightly before adjusting to his efforts.

Gant dismissed what doctors were telling him, he knew he needed surgery, but that would mean the third floor would find out. The one thing that he didn't want was for the brass to find a reason to force him off the job. Grey hairs were in season and the Police Chief made no bones about it, he had little use for older officers. Everyone in the department knew it was bullshit, but when the administration gets it in their head that experience is useless, you just can't argue with that kind of stupid.

Gant had forgotten how long he'd been hiding his health problems. Thirty-five years of eight-hour details and the constant weight of 35 pounds of equipment around his waist was the likely culprit. Pausing for a moment, he stared at the small shaving mirror hanging inside his locker. His eyes traced the silver streaks of grey in his hair flowing like a river along the side of his head and down the back of his sun browned neck.

"You're not getting old," he whispered to himself, and repeated the refrain over and over trying to make himself believe the words. It was a poor attempt at self-hypnosis. The long years in the profession had taught him to lie effortlessly and, now, the skillfulness of his lying came without effort. There were no tell-tale stutters or long uncomfortable pauses. So practiced was he that any lie he told resembled the truth and it usually worked, but not this time.

The slow betrayal of his body dragged him back to reality. There were no lies that could hide the fact that he was losing the battle of time. Rubbing his right hip with one hand, he took a few steps forward as his legs creaked like old wooden planks that had too much weight on them. Ignoring the pain, he slammed the locker shut and quickly walking away before coming to an abrupt halt. Thunderbolts of light flashed in front of his eyes and ripples of prickly agony spread out in all directions of his brain. The sound reverberated in his head like a stone being thrown into a calm lake.

"Goddammit!" he cursed his forgetfulness. A morning

hangover was not to be trifled with. Gathering what was left of his senses and equipment he headed off to the Service Division. His tour of duty had begun.

OPERATIONS DIVISION — White noise filled the squad bay until there was no space for anything else. Voices from more than a dozen conversations, each its own orchestra with squeaky highs, baritone lows, and the occasional booming of reverb seemed to come from every direction at once. The mixture of laughter and arguments made up the crazy quilt of shop talk that was policing. No single conversation could be clearly heard over the waterfall of voices, not that it mattered. Seldom was there anything interesting or factual being said.

Cops learned early to steer clear of work gossip. Wisdom dictated to keep your opinions in your back pocket and never mind the politics of the day. The police culture seldom allowed for divergence from that philosophical course. Better not to rock the boat.

"Hey Gant, you going out looking like that?" Officer Turner said with a smirk.

Gant could feel every eye in the squad room upon him. *What the hell does he care what I'm wearing?* he thought. Immediately, he took inventory of his clothing. Perhaps in his semi-sober state he'd forgotten something. His eyes scanned his uniform taking mental inventory of every piece. Gun!

His hand frantically clawed at his side holster. Feeling the cool hardness of steel, his heart slowed down and he exhaled. "Nope, got that one," he said to himself.

"What the hell are you talking about Turner?" said Gant.

Turner was of Indian descent, a fact that earned him the tag of: Steve Margaret (Hawaii five-O). He was a good cop and his sense of humor and practical joking were legendary in the department. Turner pointed toward the corkboard at the far end of the room.

"You missed something pal," Turner said, his eyes filled with tears of amusement.

Looking at the corkboard, Officer Gant's heart sank. "Can't be! It just can't be! They wouldn't do this crap to me again!" he shrieked.

There wasn't an officer who hadn't been there before. The plain truth was that blueberries loved to watch the slow burn and explosion of their fellow officers. It was horrible when it happened to you, but when it happened to someone else it was prime-time, delicious evil.

Gant wiped his eyes with his arm trying desperately to focus his blurry vision. He had glasses but had allowed the prescription to lapse to the point that they were all but useless.

Gant noticed all those little things, those tiny pinpricks of forgetfulness reminding him of what he'd lost and it became more frequent as the years passed. It was one more stone weight in the bucket of retirement. Stepping closer to the corkboard, he reluctantly read the following: *Officer Gant - In-Service Training 09:00 a.m. All officers are required to bring their bulletproof vests to the range.*

Rubbing a burly hand across his face which formed a perfect "V" at the base of his chin, he said, "Son-of-a-bitch!"

A muffled eruption of snickers and grins came from fellow officers. Everyone knew just how much Gant hated in-service training. Snatching the notice from the corkboard and crinkling the paper in a tight ball, a final curse of misfortune escaped Gant's twisted lips.

"I hate this stupid shit. I HATE IT!" Gant screamed as he stormed off toward the locker room. A teapot of steaming, hysterical laughter boiled over spilling into the squad room and the fuming officer's ears.

The pilgrimage to the range area, though familiar, took longer than usual. Gant had made up his mind that if he was going to have to endure this indignity of in-service training, he would do it on his own terms. The training was mandatory for blueberries since weapons training was one of those skills that if neglected could mean your death or another's. It was familiar. The various insects attacked in their usual D-Day attack formations, bayonets at the ready. Ticks couldn't wait to practice their Olympic pole vaulting skills upon the unsuspecting, and one needed to employ the defensive tactic of serpentine movement which seldom worked.

The blood sucking ninja-ticks were everywhere. Damn them. No matter when they scheduled in-service training, the bugs seemed to get the memo before we did and they lay in wait until we arrived. As usual, the customary rain shower soaked everything. The combination of insects and heavy rains made you believe that you'd stumbled into the Amazon rain forest. Then there was the sweltering heat, all of which turned the range into that special form of hell that only police officers and Sandinista terrorists would endure.

A gaggle of officers greeted Officer Gant as he exited his car. He slung his duty holster over his shoulder and sat begrudgingly at the ammo table. Stopping for a moment, he couldn't shake the feeling that he was missing something, something important that he'd left behind. It happened from time to time, an itch, a shard of memory at the back of his mind that refused to come into focus. What was it? Shrugging his head, Gant surrendered to the frustration. It was too early in the morning to think about this crap — *slap!*

"Jesus!"

There it was. The insect's first strike! Gant had been so distracted in his thoughts that he'd forgotten to raise his air defenses.

"Goddamned, blood-sucking mother—" he screamed.

The Worcester Police firing range was notorious for its misquote attacks. The creatures flew in "V" formations swooping down upon the hapless. Officers retaliated with bio-chemicals breaking out various types of *Deep Woods Off* sprays. The war had begun.

"Alright, everyone, gather around!" Officer Abbot's baritone voice was strict and commanded attention. In fact, everything that Abbot did came with an air of professionalism and military bearing. When he spoke, you never questioned what you were told. You just did it without hesitation.

Abbot had the dual responsibilities of range instructor and academy trainer. There wasn't a police officer on the force who didn't respect his experience and knowledge. Unfortunately, there were far too many instances where there weren't enough officers like him on the force. Speak to any police officer around the country, they would tell you that it wasn't the job that they hated, it was the uncaring, arrogant idiots running the place.

Job dissatisfaction usually flowed from the administration, top down. It was easy enough to spot, you only have to ask a simple question, "What have you done and are you doing to improve your men's morale?"

After you asked that question, you could sit back with a bowl of popcorn and watch the brass twist themselves into knots. It was one of those sad realities of policing. The people at the top of organizations never considered morale an important element of productivity. Stupid? Yeah, but this was police administration and most of the motivation to get to those positions had nothing to do with making the job better. It was all about getting more financial security and power to screw with people in the department. Petty? Small? Guilty on all accounts. Imagine a Chief of Police using hir or her power to go after another cop even after they had left the department. A lieutenant once told me, "There are no choirboys in law enforcement, plenty of hypocrites, just no choir boys."

Officer Abbot gathered us into a semi-circle and said, "When everyone's finished getting ammo, you'll break down into three lines of fire. Make sure that you have a target in front of you."

Abbot pointed to the targets mounted on wooden frames and fifty yards away. Officers lined up on the firing line at the instruction of the range officers. Officer Gant moved into position and prepared to fire. But as he did, there it was again, that itch, that unspoken thing just on the tip of his mind that he'd forgotten something. The thought itched more than the half a dozen or more red dots which freckled his arm and neck. It almost became unbearable but he just couldn't place what it was.

"Line ready!' shouted Officer Abbot. "Aim! Fire!"

Sulfur and smoke filled the air in a low-hanging cloud of destruction. The line of police officers simultaneously firing and striking simulated stationary targets was an impressive sight. The familiar pops as tiny lead projectiles with the speed of lightning found their marks, sparks of splintered wood, and paper flew like bursting fireworks. Then, a brief pause of silence which was pierced by a lone cry of agony and despair.

"Noooo!"

The scream came from the center of the firing line. In an instant, every eye turned and focused on the source of the outburst and what appeared to be a plume of green and white confetti.

The cloud of paper spread out from the single officer who had shrieked.

"What the hell is that? What is that?" yelled Officer Abbot as he sprinted to the location of the disruption. Upon his arrival at the very center of the firing line, there sat Officer Gant who had crumpled to the ground in a heap of disorganized dismay.

"Can't be! It just isn't fair," mumbled Gant.

"What's not fair? Let me see that weapon," ordered Abbot.

Sheepishly, Officer Gant passed the weapon over to the range cadre. Upon close inspection of the weapon, small minute traces of paper residue mixed with burned powder could be seen. Abbot rubbed his right temple in utter disbelief.

"What did you have in this barrel? Paper?" Abbot's tone was none too polite.

Officer Gant had no choice but to come clean. The deed was done. "Um… well, you see… ah. You know that clothing allowance check we get every year?" Abbot nodded in agreement. "Well, my wife doesn't know I get that check, so every year I have to find places to hide it from her and…" Gant's voice trailed off to a whisper.

"Wait a minute! Wait a minute!" Abbot's voice notably rose two octaves. "Are you telling me you stuffed your check inside the barrel of your weapon, then came to my range with this nonsense just to keep your clothing check a secret from your wife?" Somehow when Officer Abbot repeated the story, it sounded even more ridiculous.

"Yes…" replied Gant.

"Gant, I am going to take a sharpie pen and write *stupid* on your forehead and *ass* on the back of your head. That way, when you walk by people, they will be able to call you by your proper police name. Get the hell off my range!" Abbot screamed.

"Ah… can I get my weapon back?" Gant asked sheepishly. The question was met with glaring rage.

"What the hell do you think? You got two minutes to get off my range and out of my sight and a minute and a half of that is gone!"

There was no mistaking the tone or the intention, and Gant quickly performed a strategic retreat. In the following days, several reports had to be written and apologies made to the in-service training staff. After a while, Officer Gant was given back his weapon along with stern warnings and frequent weapons inspections.

Officer Gant even apologized to Officer Abbot for his part in the disruption of the training for that day. All of it was received well, almost too well.

Several weeks passed and Gant totally forgot about the matter. A new check would be issued by the city for his clothing allowance, but for some reason it was slow getting to him. The answer to that question would come later in the day, after his usual morning shift.

Gant had married early in his career and the love of his life, Shelly, was a proud southern woman who knew what she was marrying into. She had married a police officer. Most girlfriends and wives had to be initiated into the profession. There were stresses both on and off the job that family members had to understand and be alert for. Gant, upon entering his home was greeted by his loving wife who just happened to be waiting for him.

"Hi honey! Come on, I have a surprise for you," said Shelly.

"A surprise? What kind of surprise?" Gant immediately felt uneasy. What surprise could she be talking about? The last time she told him she had a surprise for him there was a bun in the oven.

Gant sat on the couch as his loving wife opened a curtain that covered the front main window and hastily went out of the back door.

"Keep watching the front window," she shouted over her shoulder.

"But, what?" Gant excitedly shifted on the couch unable to sit still. In a few moments, his wife appeared honking the horn of what appeared to be a brand-new Dodge Ram truck. Gant sprung to his feet!

"Wait a minute!" he spurted and ran outside to meet his wife. "Honey… did you buy me a new truck? I love you!"

Just as he attempted to open the driver's side door, his wife pushed the automatic locks on all the doors effectively locking him out.

"Honey, you ah… locked the doors," a puzzled Gant said. "I can't get in. You need to press the button to unlock the—"

Mrs. Gant twirled the car keys on a single finger. "Oh, you won't be needing to get into MY TRUCK! You see, my love, I had a conversation with a few of the wives of your fellow officers and they told me all about the range incident. Not to mention all those clothing allowance checks you've been keeping for yourself. Since we agreed to share everything fifty-fifty, I decided that my fifty was just enough to buy me this."

Shelly peered over the top of a pair of black Ray-Ban shades which she slowly pushed back over the bridge of her nose with a middle finger aimed at her husband.

Gant shrunk. "But… but… but…" was the only word salad he could manage. He was busted and he knew it. Shelly grinned from ear to ear.

"You know, honey, you are so cute when you stammer on so… two butts make an ass. We'll talk about it more when I get back, which should be in about a week or so. I've decided to take a trip with all that extra money I have leftover, and since we ARE KEEPING SECRETS from one another, I wouldn't want to spoil mine. I'll call you when I get to where I am going. There are some TV dinners in the fridge. TTFN."

The cruelest of smirks formed at the corners of Shelly's mouth as she mashed the gas pedal to the floor. A gigantic, black cloud of dust and smoke was all that was left in her wake. Officer Gant could do nothing but watch in befuddled embarrassment. Then, a horrifying thought occurred to him, *What does she mean EXTRA MONEY? We don't have any extra—*

"Sweet Jesus!" he screamed before running into the house. Sitting at the family computer, he frantically logged into their bank account.

"Please don't let it be true, please don't let it be true," he mumbled over and over again until the screen finally came into focus.

It was a dagger to his wallet. His dear, beloved Shelly had taken the exact amount of money he had been hiding from her all these years and with interest. It explained the purchase of the truck with an additional fifteen thousand dollars. Gant stared at the screen before slowly clicking the off-button. Officer Gant learned several valuable lessons in the weeks that followed:

ONE: Never lie to your wife about money, especially clothing allowances.

TWO: Don't put money in the barrel of your gun.

THREE: Never, ever depend on the brotherhood to keep a secret. They may as well be the hooded brothers.

FOUR: Don't buy any goddamned TV dinners! A week of eating that stuff will have you screaming like a samurai warrior on the toilet.

Chapter Twelve

A Side Order of Whoop Ass

A woman appeared from behind a curtain, her strapless, black chiffon evening dress flowing like a cloud, and her Prada shoes the perfect finishing touch. It was the perfect coordination of color and form, a soft shade of off-black and colors that augmented her impeccable hairstyle. Encircling her neck was a string of crystal pearls each reflecting tiny specks of silver sparkles. A gaggle of flashbulbs burst like fireworks against the backdrop of velvet darkness. A spotlight traced the women's movements to a familiar, yet unnoticed 'X' marked on the stage floor. Every eye was on her, throngs of observers from every corner of society, each waiting to see what she would do next. Some liked what she did, while others did not. Inevitably, there were those who would cynically question: *Why did she choose to do that?* It was a familiar pattern that repeated and accompanied every performance. She was, after all, on a world stage. This big stage came with invisible strings, and was the continual judgment of those who hardly know her.

Everyone told her that it came with the profession, and she believed it because it helped make sense of the harsh craziness. The complements were often offset by the numerous recriminations. She would bitterly remember it long after she stopped performing in front of them. No one saw the nervousness inside, the fear, the uncertainty, a tootsie-roll wrapper all smartly packaged, tamped down by the instruments of her profession. Slowly, she drew the bow across the strings, sound flooded the room, the performance had begun.

Policing was like that. There was a constant audience, watching, and judging the performance. They were looking for one single mistake, a missed note, or a misplayed constitutional string, any perceivable flaw the subject of scandal. That was the world of law enforcement, hard and ruthless upon those who enforced it, and mistakes were seldom tolerated. You had to be inhumanly precise, flawlessly and technically perfect when in reality you were neither and never would be. Just as in the live performance of the musician, police officers had to understand the tempo of the work. There were subtle and unique differences inherent to a particular shift. The cast of characters you met during the day differed wildly from those you encountered at night. It was said that, "Every shift represents three distinct police departments, each has its own unique problems to overcome."

There was a minefield that police officers learned to navigate, and failure to adjust could mean the difference between a pat on the back, or a bullet in the head.

There weren't many officers I liked working with, fewer still that liked working with me. I counted myself extremely lucky to have worked with Officer James Duffy despite being in different sectors of the city. Duffy had a way with people which should be (in my opinion) a requirement for the job. He was easygoing when he had to be and always knew how to keep things in perspective even in the most dangerous of situations. I grew to admire that in him, his ability to resolve a situation merely by thinking through it when others would just charge in guns-a-blazing.

In short, James Duffy was one damned, good street cop, funny as hell one minute and unshakably serious the next. I learned early in my career that a major part of working well with other blueberries had to do with your personal policing philosophy. The way a police officer worked had to be compatible with other officers. If it wasn't, you would find yourself in a *sanctioned situation* (more on that one later).

The squad room briefing was simple and to the point. The city manager was on a warpath and complaints were mounting about the rise in crime rates in the Main South area of the city of Worcester. Residents demanded something be done about it. The police were being deployed in two- and four-man teams to put an end to it. Streetwalkers and other criminal types were accosting people and robbing them at knifepoint. The prostitution circus would have made Barnum and Bailey proud, and there were more Johns taking more turns than a doorknob.

The uptick in police presence gave a false security blanket to politicians and the community alike. Every official and police officer worth their salt knew a seldom, unspoken truth: *Police presence merely displaces crime, it doesn't stop or even deter it.* Unfortunately, when politicians screamed in your ear and the manager jumped up and down pounding his desk in a monkey fit, you threw him the banana and displaced like a mother.

After the ordeal in the squad room, we hitched a ride from one of the squad cars. I soon found myself walking the length of Main South on the lookout for criminal activity. I recalled the water stories of the old-timers talking about pounding the beat. I never understood what they meant until that night.

I purchased a new pair of low-cut shoes, reasoning it would make walking a lot easier on my feet. I couldn't have been more wrong. The shoes were new and as such were stiff and needed to be broken in. After a couple of hours, my feet were on fire! Each step an agonizing exercise in Klingon pain tolerance. The urgency of that footwear change was interrupted by the immediate trouble which found us.

This trouble came in the form of a rather muscular, apparently agitated Latino male. During our travels I had been observing him from a distance, standing at the street corner, glaring at us in a not too welcoming manner. Officer Duffy noticed him too, and his body language caught both our attentions.

Body language and the ability to interpret it was a skill which was best developed through attentive study. Experience in dealing with a wide variety of people took time, and you couldn't learn it in a book. The observation of the habits, cultures, socialization and their role in police interactions was a critical policing skill. The one thing I always found alarming was that most police academies didn't teach these skills. Most learned from senior officers who passed on the knowledge if you were lucky.

Once, I had the displeasure of speaking to a Worcester police officer about his handling of four Latino males. The officer had stopped the young men during a street encounter. I was passing through the area when he called out with four subjects. Upon my arrival, I noticed that he had the youths, ages 16 to 20, lined up against a building and firing questions at them. More than once, he yelled at them about not looking him in the eye which he perceived as a slight. The officer was of proud Italian descent, and in his culture, not looking someone of authority in the eye was a sign of disrespect.

However, what the officer failed to realize was that in many Latin cultures staring figures of authority in the eyes was considered a disrespectful challenge. In other words, the officer's *cultural ignorance* led him to perceive a slight where none existed.

I pulled the officer aside and had a brief conversation with him, which he simply brushed off as me not knowing a god-damned thing. I still believe to this day, had I not arrived on that scene, there would have been arrests. Luckily, the situation was defused, and the young men were sent on their way without further incident. I got some very unwelcome stares from more than a few officers at that scene, some who carried that hate until the day I left the department. Others refused to even go to calls with me if it could be helped – *sanctioned!*

The closer we got to the subject the more irritated he became. The subject then placed his right hand deep in his pocket. In police work, you learned to pick up and be alert on subtleties. When we had gotten within thirty-five feet, it clicked. I recognized the subject from bulletins posted in the squad room. Mr. Guterez was a well-known regular in the police department, and his street reputation was made by fighting police officers. In furtherance of this goal, Mr. Guterez employed a rather sneaky method of attack. The tried-and-true *sucker punch*, which he employed numerous times to devastating effect.

There was no mistaking his hatred of the police, and it was common knowledge that he frequently carried a knife. The observation of his hand in his pocket as we drew closer took on a more urgent significance. Guterez's jaw tightened, his eyes narrowed into thin slits, and his body tensed as we approached. I noted that he had stopped leaning on the side of the building and was now in a modified ready-to-fight stance.

"Do you recognize him?" I asked, looking at Duffy for a long moment. If he heard me, he never acknowledged it, so focused was he on Guterez.

Finally, after what seemed to be an eternity he said, "Yeah, I see him. It's Guterez. You know about him, right? The *knife thing*?" Duffy's voice had an emphasis to it.

I nodded.

Twenty feet now separated us from Guterez. There was a familiar pounding in my ears, and my cop sense began kicking in. A knot the size of my fist formed in my stomach. Cotton balls of apprehension traffic jammed a third of the way down my throat. These moments wore on you. It was like revving the motor of a new car until it redlines, then repeating it every day over and over again. Tension-smashing the gas pedal to the floor, and pushing the oil pressure until the seals almost give way. Imagine it, every day for thirty years or more you beat on that engine hoping it won't fail or explode until it does (heart attack). Cops doing the job were like that car, trying not to break, not to come apart, not to explode. Unlike cars, however, there was no place to get a tune-up, or replace a faulty valve – maybe there should be.

"Let's cross here, I don't trust the sneaky bastard," I said.

Duffy nodded in agreement. There was no need to close range with this muff. The last thing either of us wanted was to give Guterez the ability to attack without warning. Stopping just fifteen feet from where the subject stood, we crossed to the other side of the empty street. Smart or stupid? Cowardly or cunning?

I learned, a long time ago from my training officer, that answering that question could be the difference between going home at the end of the shift or laying in the morgue with a toe tag. Cop sense or nonsense.

"Hey… where the fuck are you going man?" Guterez yelled.

That was it, confirmation, he was looking for a confrontation and neither of us was going to oblige.

"You fucking guys, where you going?" he yelled.

After years of serving in the Worcester Police Department, you learned a few things about dealing with people like this. If you showed them that you were afraid, it only emboldened them, and they would keep coming at you like a boulder rolling downhill. You didn't want to play squash the blueberry with these types.

I consider myself very fortunate to have learned from one of the best street cops on the job, an old-timer known as *The Stick*. Officer Vincent Turner's exploits were legendary in the department, especially when dealing with multiple attackers or rather large perpetrators, many of which he quickly dispatched with his service baton. *(Note to self - If you are ever faced with a street brawl or the Zombie Apocalypse, make sure* The Stick Turner *is your backup.)*

In my conversations with *The Stick*, he told me something that I would never forget, and I put that advice into practice during my career. He said, *"The secret to dealing with big, tough customers is simple. Make sure they believe you're nuttier than they are. You have to sell them on the idea, you'll go that extra mile into crazy-town with them. If they believe you, they won't want any part of you. This method can be an effective way of deescalating a bullying situation."*

Officer Turner's advice proved to be correct many times over. The older officers, the ones who had been on the street for some time, had pearls of wisdom you can't get in a book or an academy.

I guess that's how they got to be old-timers. It was also the reason why you needed that experience in a department, and you should never just push them out the door. Get rid of the dinosaurs, they're too old? They have nothing to contribute? Grey hairs? Administrators and officers who thought this way suffered from constipation of the brain, resulting in diarrhea of the mouth. How the hell did they think these officers survived long enough to get them gray hairs?

Experience and wisdom had a place in the puzzle of policing, and it was good practice to remember that. Anyone from the Chief of Police on down who didn't understand this wasn't deserving of the rank or position. Wisdom had its place in training and reducing future lawsuits due to mistakes of the head.

"What the hell is wrong with you?" I said, mustering my most menacing voice. "You'd BETTER stop all that god-damned yelling and screaming. I don't have time for your bullshit tonight, Guterez."

Mr. Guterez stood frozen just staring blankly. I surmised he wasn't accustomed to police officers speaking to him that way.

"Do you know who the fuck I am?" he asked.

"Yeah, we know who you are. The fool who likes sucker punches." Duffy replied.

"Look, I just told you I don't have time for your silly shit tonight. Go on your way," I said sternly.

"You think I'm a piece of shit, don't you?" Guterez said.

INTERNAL THOUGHT — *Now, that was a loaded question. The fact was that being a police officer was like being a roll of toilet paper in a room full of assholes. You just knew that sooner or later someone was going try to wipe their ass with you.*

"I don't like cops. What if I feel like being an asshole with you?" Guterez sneered.

It was at these times that verbal judo should and must be employed. I quickly formulated a response.

"I wouldn't advise it. I always keep a bottle of asshole pills for just such an occasion, you don't want me to open it. I absolutely guarantee you, his is not going down the way you think." I glared back without blinking.

There was a long, tense moment where time seemed to stop. I observed his eyes which turned upward and to the right. That body language meant that he was thinking, considering the alternatives, and that was a good thing. If a suspect was thinking, it meant he was not acting and hadn't formulated a plan. Guterez, without a single word, abruptly turned and walked away in the opposite direction, but I noticed that his hand never left his pocket. The possible crisis was averted for now. In policing you had to know when to back down and when to backup. In the profession and on the beat, it was hard to do sometimes. Often, police officers felt they had to win every confrontation, be it physical or verbal. But you didn't — you just didn't.

In study guides for promotional exams, it was emphasized that: *The most preferred result of a criminal encounter is an arrest...* While this advice might at first seem sound, in fact, it was the worst crap you can possibly tell a police officer. It meant: *Don't be a problem solver. Arrest!*

If you didn't want to think too hard about the solution then, arrest! If you didn't want to back down or backup because big, brave, macho police never do that, then arrest! I can tell you from twenty-eight years of policing experience that this attitude was what got police officers in the most trouble, and sometimes killed.

The police didn't have to win every argument, but every fight... hell yeah, you gotta win those! Not every argument though. Policing was always a thinking man's or woman's game. Police didn't need to dive headlong into confrontation just because we had become emotionally compromised. I had always instructed those who I trained to solve the problems and not create them. The last thing you wanted was to become some muffs blue lottery ticket.

In the case of Mr. Guterez, our encounter wasn't criminal. It hedged on disorderly conduct if you wanted to stretch the facts *(creative writing = lie)*. Blueberries relied on the teachings of the *Force Continuum*. This theory taught officers (rightly so) to react to threats. But what it didn't teach officers was how to keep an encounter from spiraling out of control. Problem-solving techniques were not emphasized in most departments. In the end, this lack of training could lead to sketchy arrests or death over a trivial matter. What would modern policing be if we arrested people merely because we didn't like what they said to us? I mean, citizens from around the country would be screaming for police reform — *Umm... isn't that what's happening now?*

Keeping our distance, we continued on our assignment mostly without incident, that is until a call for help crackled over the radio.

"Dispatch, we're out with a Latino male at— Hey! Wait! Put your hands up! I said, step the hell back— get back— Ahh!" screamed the officer. The radio transmission ended, dropping into a bucket of silence. Not good...

I stared at Officer Duffy, my mouth hinged open, recalling the events earlier in the evening.

"Hey, Duffy, doesn't that sound like our friend from—"

Duffy knew what I was talking about. "Yep… we better start heading that way."

Officer Martin and Green weren't new to the job, in fact, they had almost seven years of service. They graduated near the top of their respective academy classes and were considered to be promising police officers. In only their third year, they had both manage to get accepted to the SWAT Team. This was no simple task as the teams were often very selective and required the most severe physical training and conditioning. The officers made good decisions on the streets, were by the book, and were known for their exceptional work ethic.

On this particular summer's night, both would take their turn at the gaming table. As it was with every police officer, it always came down to choice. When the dice of fate rolled, you hoped it came up seven or eleven. The pair could have chosen to walk on Main Street or they could have turned right onto Wellington Street and continued their foot patrol.

Left or right, a roll of the dice — they chose to take a right onto Wellington Street. This put them straight in the path of a man-mountain of trouble in the form of Mr. Guterez *(craps)*. The unsuspecting pair passed within arm's reach of the subject when a burly fist abruptly and without warning punched one of them in the face. Officer Green crumple to the ground like a spilled bag of potato chips, clutching his bloodied mouth. Officer Martin had only seconds to compose himself. Instinctively, he lunged forward grabbing Guterez by the arms.

The officer realized too late that the high humidity of the evening made holding onto bare skin nearly impossible. The table was tilted in favor of Guterez. He grabbed the horrified officer by the collar, lifting him effortlessly off the ground. The officer struggled as an ant might when placed under a magnifying glass. In one fluid motion, Guterez whirled him to the right, slamming officer Martin into a nearby chain-link fence.

Officer Green staggered to his feet still groggy from the blow, but managed to place a frantic call for help. Soon, foot patrol cruisers were speeding to his location. Guterez then turned his attention back to Officer Green who by this time had drawn his baton. Bracing one leg forward and the other back, Green prepared to deliver what he hoped would be a disabling blow. Guterez charged like a mad bull. The officer stood his ground. One might admire the bravery if not for the pure foolish futility of the act. Guterez was three times the size and weight of the young officer. Officer Green had as much chance of winning as a bug had with the windshield of a speeding car. Predictably, the officer met with the same fate. Guterez collided with the Officer Green driving him savagely backward and to the ground like a railroad tie.

It was just at this moment that a single officer arrived. Exiting his cruiser, he quickly entered the fray. Officer Tate drew his baton and delivered a terrific blow squarely to the knee and thigh area of the man-mountain. Guterez stopped— for a moment time froze. He looked down at the baton in the officer's hand, then at his knee. Slowly, hate filled eyes traced an imaginary path from the officer's baton to the hand that held it. Shortly thereafter, his eyes came to rest upon the face of the stunned officer. A sinister grin slowly emerged.

"Is that all you got?" he whispered. It was at this exact moment that Officer Tate fully understood the meaning of the phrase, *Pucker Factor*.

This event occurred when a police officer realized that being in a street brawl is akin to having an umbrella shoved up your backside and then opened. Fear took hold, and so did Officer Martin who had recovered enough to jump on Mr. Guterez's back, coiling his arms around the suspect's massively muscled neck. Guterez reached above and behind his head peeling Officer Martin off like an onion skin. Grabbing the officer by the shirt and tie, he began a rapid windshield wiper slapping action (back and forth, back and forth). It wasn't going well for the three officers, at least that was the assessment of the additional arriving officers.

The four additional officers waded into the police scrum, three of which were SWAT team members. Guterez was in mid-swing when the officers jumped on his back and shoulders only to be quickly thrown off. The officers regrouped and charged madly at their antagonist in the hopes that the sheer weight of numbers would overpower the suspect. All that this accomplished was a gaggle of blue getting in each other's way so that none but Guterez had clear control. Almost as quickly as Guterez would throw one officer off of his back, another would replace him. It was a wild scene that met the eyes of arriving officials as no less than seven officers fought to subdue the combative, individual man-mountain.

Guterez, undeterred by the numerical superiority of blue, hoisted one officer high into the air before launching him up and over the hood of a nearby cruiser. Soon, superior numbers and fatigue, however, did what no singular officer could accomplish. Guterez crumpled to the ground under a mass of exhausted police officers. It took four officers, two on each arm, to get the suspect's hands behind his massive back. So muscular were his arms and shoulders that four sets of handcuffs had to be linked together to finally get the suspect shackled, finally bringing the brawl to an end. Scattered about the sidewalk lay a battleground of police personal items, hats, batons, wallets, and glasses. There were ripped shirts and pants. Hurricane Guterez left nothing but devastation in his wake as he continued to curse the officers.

I arrived with Officer Duffy as the wagon was arriving. We had been so far away that it took us a long time to get to the location. Upon seeing myself and Officer Duffy, Officer McGrath sprinted over to where we were standing.

"Where? WHERE WERE YOU GUYS?" he yelled. "We called for help, where were you?" His voice trembled, obviously shaken from the encounter.

"We were coming from a distance," I said. "You had seven cops, fourteen sets of cuffs, seven canisters of pepper spray, seven batons, four SWAT team members, and 252 bullets. Jesus, you had everything but a partridge in a pear tree. How many cops do you need to take down one guy?" I said with a half-grin.

The Captain and Sergeant could hardly restrain their laughter as Duffy and I turned away doing our level best to hide our devilish grins and muffled snickers.

Sometimes, when the police dealt with the public, we got served a side order of whoop-ass. It just happened that that was a part of the job we never advertised. I and Officer Duffy went home without a single scratch that night. We both chalked up our good fortune to the grey-haired experience.

Chapter Thirteen

Aluminum Foil

All was fine until my Ford began to smoke and sputter before finally rolling to a complete stop. I couldn't understand it, I'd just gotten it out of the shop and there was plenty of gas. Yet, there I was in the middle of some of the most scenic countryside anywhere, broke down, and with no damned cell signal. I got out the of car cursing my misfortune when I noticed a single farmhouse across a field of waist-high blue wheat. I began walking toward the structure, reasoning that I might find a sympathetic Samaritan or at the least a phone to get a tow.

Wading into the blue wheat, I saw several dairy cows grazing, the view reminded me of a vibrant colored painting. I continued to walk toward the house and when I looked again, there were six cows grazing. I could have sworn there were only two moments before. I focused on the farmhouse, but for some unexplained reason, I found my attention drawn to the grazing herd. Something was disquieting about them. The number of cows was growing and they all seemed to be watching me, slowly following me. It was simply unnatural, and I quickened my pace. To my surprise, the bovines increased their pace to a trot and rapidly closed in on me.

Fear took hold as I began to jog, then sprint toward the farmhouse. The evil bovines were gaining on me I could feel the ground tremble, their hot breath steaming toward me. I ran faster still, staggering through the wheat which seemed to be clutching at me, inhibiting me with every step. I tripped and the beasts were fully upon me. Rolling to the left, a hoof came crashing down on what would have been my skull had I been but an instant slower. I then rolled to my right, avoiding yet another calamity. How could this be happening? What the hell is going on here? These damned Jerseys were trying to kill me! Instinctively, I reached down to my waistband for my gun, only to find I was in my underwear? Where the hell were my clothes? Where was my gun?

Suddenly, strong arm… err… hooves pinned me down, and I couldn't move however much I struggled. The herd formed a Mayan circle around my prone form and stared menacingly at me through bloodshot eyes.

"Let me go, goddamn it! Let me go!" I roared.

A chorus of moos arose from the herd, only to be interrupted by a rising crescendo. A dark evil chant flooded my senses like an overflowing river.

"Milk him! Milk him! Milk Him! Milk Him!"

The chant grew louder and louder until it thundered in my brain, "MILK HIM! MILK HIM! MILK HIM!"

I thought my eardrums were going to burst when an impressive Jersey cow whose form was much larger than the rest made her way toward me.

"Silence!" she ordered. "Tis I who be doin' the milking here!" she proclaimed, and the herd immediately fell silent. Her eyes were like two large disks of black obsidian boring into my soul. I averted my gaze from that horrid bovine or I would have surely drowned in those dark, liquid orbs. I squirmed and writhed under my captures grasp, struggling to break the bonds which held me, but to no avail.

"Let me go! What do you want from me?" I screamed.

"Tis a lesson we be teaching ye 'bout challenging one of our own. Let it begin!"

To my eternal horror, the evil bovine queen positioned herself directly over me, her utters mere inches from my face. Then, she lowered those devilish dairy daggers upon my now screaming countenance, smothering me. I gasped and gaged, clawing for air. Again and again, she raised and forcefully lowered those massive, balloon-like repositories on my face. Suddenly, there was a loud whooshing noise, and I was mercilessly hosed down by gallons and gallons of warm milk. I couldn't breathe! Buckets of milk covered my eyes, face, and nose choking me. Gasping, and sputtering milk everywhere, I screamed and fought against the hooves that restrained me! Until—

I opened my eyes and was greeted by an impenetrable darkness. My throat was fully constricted, and I couldn't breathe. In an absolute state of panic, I clutched the blankets which had covered and entangled my head and arms and raked them away in frantic desperation. Perspiration dripped from my face as I gulped in sweet mouthfuls of air. My heart rate began to slow and the mist of fear lifted as my eyes began to focus. The farm house, the pasture, those damned devilish bovines and their queen were gone. All that remained was my dimly lit bedroom. I fell backward onto a crumpled mess of pillows. A dream? A nightmare?

"Goddamned Irish Whiskey," I cursed, swinging my legs to the floor. Leaning forward, I placed my sweaty forehead in both palms and tried to rub the sleep from my eyes.

The alarm clock howled like a savage animal, making a milkshake of my already rattled senses. Damn, was it 5 o'clock already? I slapped the snooze button on the alarm then ran my tongue across my teeth. My less than pearly whites felt like the woolly sweater I'd gotten last Christmas. Looking across the room at my reflection in the mirror I cringed. "Yuck!" A white milk-like substance was running from both eyes and down the sides of my face. It looked like... a cow had sat on my— Nah! Just a dream, right? I chuckled inwardly at the absurdity of it all. Still, the thought lingered longer than it should have.

My whole body creaked like a rusty gate. Every joint of my body ached. It was the price I paid for hanging out with the rest of the recruits celebrating our graduation. I'd never had whiskey before, but Mike O'Brien was a proud Irishman and eager to teach me the finer points of drinking Irish whiskey. I don't know what the hell I was thinking, trying to match drinks with him. The matter, however, was closed and I was paying the price with a hangover the size of the Grand Canyon. My head throbbed as I steadied myself at the bathroom sink. It was then that I realized just how lethal beer breath mixed with whiskey can be.

The odor emanating from my pie-hole was nothing short of alarming. The funk bared a close resemblance to the pungent fragrance one might encounter if you should happen to be munching on dusty Himalayan Yak ass. Holding my breath, I grabbed the tube of Colgate and went to work attacking the yak.

After a good five minutes, and almost bleeding gums, I managed to stumble into the shower. The steady stream of water droplets bouncing off my skull made my head feel like a coin jar. I was ready to confess to everything and anything real or made up just to make it stop. My brain, however, found an easier solution. I took a step back and tilted my head up to relieve my bursting head, and allowed the water to wash my face. Soon, the steamy hot water soothed me and revived my senses, and I began to feel more human. I had to be operating at 100 percent today, because I would be getting evaluated by my assigned training officer.

All new recruits were assigned an FTO (Field Training Officer), and I'd be under the watchful tutelage of Officer Andrew Harris. This would be our first meeting, and I wanted to get off to a good start. I'd heard he was a hybrid mix of Denzel Washington, John Shaft, and Plato, and that meant he was clever, fearless, and smart. Drew was considered by many of his peers to be one of the best officers to train with. It was true.

I turned off the water and reached for a nearby towel when my cell phone started to ring. It was John Vassar no doubt. I'd asked him to give me a wakeup call since he was a dependable, early riser. Hands still dripping wet, I picked up the phone.

"You up?" asked John.

"Yeah, I'm awake. Thanks for the call," I said, trying my best not to sound too screwed up. It didn't work.

"You sound like crap, man. I told you not to try and out-drink an Irishman!" John retorted, his laughter echoing through the phone and delivering a perfect strike to the pins in my head before the line went dead.

I was a little ticked off, but I knew John was right. Hell, he was always right. Vassar always had a better read on people than I did. I was always too damn trusting, and I'd paid for it on more than one occasion.

I had to be at the station before 7:30, so I rushed around getting dressed. Putting on the uniform, the vest, the gun, and the badge was a ritual. Getting into the correct mindset was not only necessary, but also primordial to my survival. Cops never, ever, think that they might not come home alive, that they might just die on the job that day. It's not an option, we lie to ourselves and pretend that it's not all that dangerous. It's how blueberries cope, how I coped, how I survived. But it was a strange feeling and hard to identify, and always on the edge of my mind, or was it a voice? That nagging voice that kept pestering me is today the day I bite the dust? and eventually becoming a constant scream over the years. I didn't want to think about it, so I pushed it back as so many police officers do. We call it normal, pushing back those feelings, when we know that it's anything but normal.

Arriving at the station house, I immediately went to the

Operations Division where I met my training officer and partner for the day, Officer Andrew Harris.

"Well, you made it," said Harris, and smirked.

"Yes, Sir," I replied respectfully.

"Hey, now let's get one thing straight from the get go," Harris warned. "I am not a Sir. I work for a living and you can call me Drew, or Officer Harris, but forget the Sir shit."

That was my first conversation with Officer Harris and the one that I remember most when I think back to those amazingly satisfying, yet terrifying years of service. I came to rely on Drew's advice in the many years that followed, both on and off the job.

After gathering together endless reams of paperwork, we set off for the cruiser lot. We would be working an active area, Route 13, and were on patrol within minutes of entering the cruiser.

"Route 13?"

"Go ahead dispatcher," I responded.

"Go to 43 Marblehead Street to see a woman regarding suspicious persons… possible Peeping Tom."

"Receive in route."

Andrew gave a deep sigh and a noticeable frown crossed

his face. "Well, here we go… this will be a good call for you. Just watch what I do, okay?"

I nodded. This being my first domestic call, my heart was racing and my palms felt like I'd just gotten out of a swimming pool. We arrived at a single-family home. The yard's overgrown grass flanked the entrance, and the windows were a dingy hue of brown with enough dirt to draw a picture on. The porch had old country style wooden planks that had long since faded to a dusty grey color and gaps had formed exposing their lack of maintenance. Everywhere I looked, the house showed the telltale signs of disrepair and neglect. I followed closely behind Officer Harris as we entered and knocked on the door. I wasn't consciously holding my breath, but I wasn't breathing either as we waited.

There was the sound of someone fumbling about inside and after a long moment of silence, the door slowly creaked open just a sliver. A thin twig of a woman, barely visible through the open crack, was peering suspiciously at us with her visible eye. The door slammed shut and we heard the sound of various chain locks rattle as they were slid to the side and removed from their rails. The door was then flung fully open revealing a mere slip of an elderly woman with salt and pepper hair who I guessed to be in her early 70's. My attention, however, was drawn to her rather large blue horn-rimmed glasses which over framed her fragile features. She squinted half revealing steel grey eyes and said, "Yes, Officers, I am glad you came. Come in, come in." With a single crooked finger, the old woman motioned for us to enter.

We entered the dimly lit apartment and were immediately hit by the nauseating odor of spoiled food which hung in the air like a thick blanket assaulting our nostrils. The musty smell of mold swirled about the stale air, cigarette butts pitted the blackened low nap carpet, and a nicotine hue rested upon everything within the enclosure. The wallpaper, once white with paisley designs, was covered in a dreary brownish maple color. I tried not to let my eyes rest in any one place, and swallowed hard in a desperate attempt to suppress the involuntary gag reflex which protested the assault on my senses. On an unkempt wooden table pushed against the far wall, there was a dish of uneaten cat food. I wondered if the old woman allowed her cat to eat on her table and shuddered. Quickly, I continued my evaluation of the house and scanned the rest of the room, but found no trace of the feline, no kitty litter box, nothing to indicate the presence of a cat. Interestingly, Officer Harris seemed immune to it all and was carrying on his conversation with the women as if nothing around him mattered. How could this not be affecting him? This was not a home. It was a cave annexed from some dark part of the Brazilian rain forest, dank, dark, and smelly.

"Ma'am, you called the police about a Peeking Tom?"

Harris interjected.

"Yes I did," replied the old woman. "They have been coming to my window everyday now and spying on me. I have told them to stop it, but they won't leave me alone. I want you to do something about it."

I looked at Officer Harris puzzled and tried to ask a question, but he shook his head rebuking my question even before I spoke it.

"How long has this been going on?" asked Harris.

"It's been happening every day for over a month now, officer, and I want you to do something about it. It's not right." There was a desperateness in her crackling, high pitched voice and despite the deplorable conditions of her home, a silent voice in the back of my mind kept saying, *This could be your own grandmother.*

Anger replaced pity as I tried to imagine someone, anyone, who the heartless "they" could refer to. How dare they taunt and harass an elderly woman? It made my blood boil just thinking about it.

"Where do you see them when they come?" asked Harris.

"They usually come to that window and look in on me. They stare at me at all hours," replied the women, pointing to the living room window.

Officer Harris walked over to the window and pulled back the drab olive-green curtain. The window was covered with a shiny reflective substance. Harris nodded to himself and walked back to the old lady to continue his conversation. Since he didn't say anything to me, I wondered what exactly was on that window and stepped closer to observe for myself.

"Hey, come over here. I want you to finish taking the rest of this women's statement," Harris called out. "This will give you some experience in taking reports, and I will observe you."

REPORTS! I could hardly contain my excitement. This would be my first report with a real citizen, someone who needed the police to serve and protect. I was going to be the one to write that report and solve this case. It was over the top I know, but for a green rookie it was one of the most exciting things I had done so far. No simulation, no practice runs, this was the real deal, and I was loving it. Why then was Officer Harris grinning as he stepped behind me toward the door?

I started my interview as I had been taught, asking the standard questions until the lengthy report formalities was completed. Then, without warning, the elderly woman pointed toward the living room window.

"Officer, Look! There they are! Get out of there! Get out!" screamed the old crone.

My head swiveled in the direction of the window, but there was nothing there that I could see. Still the woman persisted.

"Get away from here! Stop watching me!" she screamed, grabbed a food encrusted dish, and flung it at the wall! "I know how to deal with you!" she retorted, and in an instant retreated to a nearby room. I looked over at Officer Harris whose grin had now morphed into a larger-than-life smile.

"Well, just don't stand there, find out what's going on," he said with a half snicker of restrained laughter.

My mind raced for a solution. This crap wasn't in the training. What the hell was going on? Before I could answer my own inner voice, however, the old woman returned wearing a makeshift aluminum foil hat, slippers wrapped in aluminum, and what appeared to be a hand cranked eggbeater. Stupefied, I watched as she moved with all the tactical stealth of a commando toward the window and began to actuate the eggbeater.

"Back, you devils!" the crone shouted! "Back to the abyss from which you came, Satan! Satan!" She then turned an evil, twisted eye in my direction.

I backed up in surprise. This call had just morphed into crazy town, and I was along for the ride. In that minimal but terrifying moment, all of my training left me. My mouth hanging open, I turned to Officer Harris seeking the solace and wisdom of his counsel. Harris, having seen the obvious confusion written all over my face, had already opened the front door and was halfway out of the apartment.

"Now, you finish that report. I'll be waiting in the car for you when you're done." The door slammed shut in his wake, and I could hear his laughter as he walked away.

I was trapped! Abandoned! Alone with this delusional, old woman who was menacingly closing in on me, her actuating, purgatory-dispersing eggbeater in hand.

"Do you see them?" she screamed. "Officer, they are everywhere! DO YOU SEE THEM?" the crone cackled.

"Yes, yes! I see them," I screamed back, more out of fear than agreement. At that moment, I would have told her that I saw the second coming of Jesus Christ just to get the hell out of that apartment. She reached out and grabbed me by the arm, her boney clutch making my skin crawl under my uniform. I staggered backward and slammed against the door, the door knob jabbing me in the lower back. She began to rave again, but I couldn't make out the words because I couldn't breathe. The foul oh-dear (odor) that emanated from her snaggle toothed countenance teared my eyes like an onion. It was an odor foul yet familiar, with just the hint of meow mix— Oh god! The dominoes fell into place in my mind and I almost gagged. She didn't have a cat. She was the one eating that cat food! All thoughts of the police report abandoned me. The only thing that mattered was escape. My eyes, now adjusted to the darkness, flashed to the windows once again. I now saw clearly, for the first time, what I did not earlier. Every window in the apartment was covered in aluminum foil, and on the ceiling, there was a drawing of a Satanic Pentagram.

"Come, come, you can help me fight them!" the old woman chimed, and shot a sly, evil grin in my direction. "But you must have a weapon! Here, let me get you some foil, it will protect you from the rays!" The old women released her grip and flew into the kitchen.

Now was my chance. Gripped with fear and sweating bullets, I turned around. While the foiled lady was distracted with her errand, I broke into full Colonel Sanders retreat. I grasped the door knob, the lower back still smarting from where it had been lodged seconds before, and flung the door open.

"That's alright! I have all I need!" I shouted over my shoulder, and ran out slamming the door shut behind me.

I was all chocolate ass and elbows as I got the hell out of there and ran full speed to the squad car. Eyes bulging, I sucked in the sweet aroma of the city air only to find Officer Harris's arms wrapped around his ribs, roaring with laughter, and tears streaming down his face.

That's when it hit me for a second time. It was a setup! A damn initiation of sorts. I was pissed!

"You should have seen your face!" Harris said, pointing at me.

"You could have told me." I shot back.

"Oh, no, some things you just have to learn for yourself," he responded between breaths.

I got into the cruiser feeling utterly embarrassed and fuming with Harris still laughing. Just as we were about to pull away from the apartment, the old women snatched the foil from the window and screamed, "Officer! Officer! When they come for you remember to yell *Moooo! Moooo!* and don't let them hold you down! Run faster!" Then, she screamed wildly and waved the eggbeater in the air as if fending off evil spirits.

Officer Harris stared at her dumbfounded. "That's new! She never did that before."

"Drive!" I shouted! "Drive! Drive!"

As we drove away, I shot a glance back over my shoulder. The old crone stared back with blank and distant eyes. The sight of her wearing that aluminum foil hat while still feverishly actuating her weaponized eggbeater would haunt my dreams for days. I can still hear her shrill, cackling voice uttering her war cry, "Moooo! Moooo!" My thoughts recalled the events from earlier that morning and I wondered, *How could she possibly know? How did she know?* The question rented permanent space in my head as I tried to push Officer Harris's jubilant laughter out of my mind.

God damned Irish Whiskey…

Message from Charles Brace:

I hope that you enjoyed reading C.O.P.S. as much as I enjoyed writing it. Before putting the book or your Kindle aside, I humbly ask that you please take a moment to leave a review on Amazon. Reader reviews are very important to me and help the books you like become more popular. Thank you!

REVIEW LINK FOR C.O.P.S.

Acknowledgments

I want to thank all those officers who were confidentially interviewed for their stories. Thank you for your continued service for justice in these most difficult times.

I also want to give a huge thank you to a distinguished author and screenwriter, Mr. Amir Bavar. If not for his constant encouragement and contributions, I may never have finished this book. Please read some of his work which can be found on Amazon.com.

Az: Revenge of an Archangel

https://www.amazon.com/dp/B00XIN9ICC

Az: Hunting the Klan

https://www.amazon.com/gp/product/B086RG8CN4

Samantha: The Haunting

https://www.amazon.com/dp/B0762H1T7W

Printed in Great Britain
by Amazon